NESTING IN THE ROCK

FINDING THE FATHER IN EACH EVENT

by

GEORGE A. MALONEY, S.J.

DIMENSION BOOKS

DENVILLE, NEW JERSEY

Imprimi Potest: Rev. Eamon Taylor, S.J.
Provincial of the New York Province
April 18, 1977

L.C.C.C. No. 77-79226
ISBN 0-87193-002-1

—Dedication—

To Ken and June Culver and their family who have shared with me their joys and sufferings and have taught me what true abandonment to God's holy will means in family life.

ACKNOWLEDGEMENTS

Deepest gratitude to Sister Joseph Agnes of the Sisters of Charity of Halifax for reading and typing this manuscript. Grateful acknowledgment is made to the following publishers: Darton, Longman & Todd, Ltd. and Doubleday & Company, Inc., N.Y. for excerpts from *The Jerusalem Bible,* copyright 1966 by Darton, Longman & Todd, Ltd., and Doubleday and Company, Inc. All scriptural texts are from *The Jerusalem Bible* unless otherwise noted. To the Institute of Carmelite Studies (ICS Publications) of Washington, D.C. for excerpts from *The Collected Works of St. John of the Cross,* tr. by Kieran Kavanaugh, O.C.D. and Otilio Rodriguez, O.C.D.

TABLE OF CONTENTS

INTRODUCTION

She lived in solitude,
And now in solitude has built her nest;
And in solitude He guides her,
He alone, Who also bears
In solitude the wound of love.[1]

Can you remember the first time, perhaps as a child, you found a bird's nest, hidden in a tree or a bush? There was a certain reverence which came over you as you peeked into the nest. Perhaps you found some eggs or, even a greater discovery, you were confronted by little birds, stretching their necks, beaks open, crying for food from their mother or father.

A nest does something to most people, at least it does so to me. It must have done so also to the Israelites in the desert, to the Psalmist, and to Jesus Himself for we read the many references in Holy Scripture to nests. Perhaps we resonate with the thought of a nest for it is one of the most primal "places" for the beginning of new life. God is described as protecting, rearing His people in the desert, "Like an eagle watching its nest . . ." (Dt 32:11).

A nest has a comforting, surrounding wall, that keeps out rain and snow, wind and cold, especially when the mother bird sits on the freshly-hatched brood of fledglings.

In the nest, life comes out of the egg where it has been encapsulated in its embryonic form. It is quite similar to the womb where a like process from embryo to full life takes place.

When, therefore, I came upon the phrase in the Book of Numbers (Nb 24:21): ". . . and your nest perched high in the rock," the many references from Holy Scripture to God and especially to Jesus Christ as the *Rock* came to mind. The Israelites understood in deserts of shifting sands the silent strength and stability of the huge rocks that make up much of the Sinai Desert. It was the most natural image to describe the fidelity and constancy of God in His loving, protective guidance of His wandering People.

Yahweh's greatness is proclaimed by Moses: "He is the Rock, his work is perfect" (Dt 32:4). God is "the Rock who begot you" (Dt 32:18). David is delivered from Saul and his enemies and he sings these words:

> Yahweh is my rock and my bastion,
> my deliverer is my God.
> I take refuge in him, my rock.
> . . . Who else is God but Yahweh,
> Who else a rock save our God?
> This God who girds me with strength
> and makes my way without blame,
> . . . Life to Yahweh! Blessed be my rock! (2 S 22:2-3, 32, 47).

Similar phrases echo through many of the Psalms (cf. Ps 18:2; 27:5; 28:1; 42:9; 62:2,6,7; 73:3; 78:35; 89:26; 92:15). Isaiah exhorts God's People to enter into the rock and hide there at the coming of the awesome Yahweh (Is 2:10).

JESUS THE ROCK

But it is St. Paul who so beautifully describes Jesus as the Rock. He refers, in 1 Co 10:3-4 to the Israelites at Kadesh when Moses struck the rock to give them life-giving waters. "And Moses raised his hand and struck the rock twice with the branch; water gushed in abundance, and the community drank and their cattle too" (Nb 20:11).

Jesus claims the role of Moses when He shouts out in the temple court on the feast of the Tabernacles:

'If any man is thirsty, let him come to me!' As scripture says: From his breast shall flow fountains of living water. He was speaking of the Spirit which those who believed in him were to receive; for there was no Spirit as yet because Jesus had not yet been glorified (Jn 7:38-39).

A whole school of exegesis stemming from Antiochene teachers in the Johannine tradition [2] interprets the saying of Jesus in such a way that from Jesus' breast (or heart) shall flow fountains of living water. The Spirit is the living waters that in Baptism come to us from the pierced heart of Jesus. Jesus is the Lamb that is slain (Rv 5:12). This is no doubt what John the Evangelist had in mind when he gives us the scene on Calvary: ". . . one of the soldiers pierced his side with a lance; and immediately there came out blood and water" (Jn 19:34).

The Holy Spirit purifies our hearts, the deepest layers of our consciousness, by revealing the love of Jesus for us in the symbol of His pierced heart. "Nesting in the Rock" is to contemplate by the power of the Spirit the infinite love of God the Father, made manifest for us in the emptied Jesus on the Cross. Centered upon Jesus and the depths of His love for us, we will be cleansed of self-centeredness. We can continuously approach this sacred fountain, the Rock that is Jesus Christ, and be washed through the Spirit's revelation of God's love in the water and blood of Christ.

St. Paul refers to the rock in the desert that gave the Israelites life-giving water but he insists that this rock went with them:

> . . . all ate the same spiritual food and all drank the same spiritual drink, since they all drank from the spiritual rock that followed them as they went, and that rock was Christ (1 Co 10:3-4).

Without saying it in so many words, this book is about contemplative prayer. It is not meant to look at contemplation separated from your living situation, but rather it is a call to go into your daily life and contemplate how Yahweh, the wonderful Heavenly Father is your Rock and Salvation. That Rock accompanies you daily through Jesus Christ, God's gift of Himself in His spoken Word. For St. Paul and for you, Jesus is always dying (Ga 2:20). He is in each moment, in each event, opening up His "heart," the depths of His love for you and again showing you the Father. "To have seen me is to have seen the Father" (Jn 14:9).

ABANDONMENT

This is also a book on *abandonment* to God's dynamic love as He works out our salvation or healing in each moment. Many books have been written in the past. One that easily will come to your mind is the classic, *Self-Abandonment to Divine Providence* by J.P. De Caussade,

S.J. Other writers like St. Francis de Sales, Bossuet, Monsignor C. Gay, St. Alphonsus Liguori and Dom Vital Lehodey have developed this same theme.

But, nevertheless, even though these works had a great influence on me, I still felt their approach was very limited, too *scholastic* and perhaps even tinged with a bit of French Jansenism. What I thought was needed was to present a trustful abandonment in more existential terms. I saw in the Greek Fathers a mysticism based on the *process* theology of the Trinity's "uncreated energies," acting in love in every atom of matter, touching us in each *event of every day.*

From a traditional exegesis from which such writers approached God, God had spoken that: "I am who am" (Ex 3:14). Much scholarly work has been done on this phrase, giving us a new and exciting understanding of God. No longer should we regard Him as static and unchanging. Thus also no longer can we consider His divine decrees as pre-determined from all eternity.

God is He who will reveal Himself to His Chosen People in their next step, in their existential lives. God is always forward and becoming God as Love in His People's needs of the next moment.

God's actions in relieving sufferings from His children reveal His true name: "I will be with you." God becomes a loving Father through His Word that is being released in our daily lives. God, through His living Word, unconceals and gathers His scattered children into a community, an *ekklesia,* His Church. We must listen each moment to hear God's Word, to discover God as loving Father and to respond as His loving children.

Through constant purification of the heart and continued *nepsis* or vigilance to be attentive to God's energizing "inbreaking" at all times, we Christians are called to "see" God in all things. We are to contemplate Him as actively loving us in everything that happens.

AN ACTIVE RESPONSE

Former writers perhaps would have been comfortable with a title such as "A Nest in the Rock." I wanted to suggest also, not only the passive acceptance of God's activities in our lives, but also our wholehearted *response* to God's call in each event. As Jesus contemplated His Heavenly Father working at all times in all circumstances (Jn 5:17), so He responded with the fullness of His being to cooperate with His Father's activities.

The Greek Fathers call it a "synergy," a working together actively, man with God, creatively to bring forth the world according to God's eternal plan. St. Paul put it in terms of our becoming new creatures in Christ Jesus through the death of the old man to be invited by God to become reconcilers of the whole world:

> It is all God's work. It was God who reconciled us to himself through Christ and gave us the work of handing on this reconciliation. In other words, God in Christ was reconciling the world to himself, not holding men's faults against them, and he has entrusted to us the news that they are reconciled. So we are ambassadors for Christ; it is as though God were appealing through us, and the appeal that we make in Christ's name is: be reconciled to God (2 Co 5:18-20).

A MYSTICISM

Mysticism or the deepest levels of contemplative prayer concern our self-abandonment to God. We can only surrender ourselves to God to the degree that we have experienced His immense, burning love for us individually. Mysticism is not a honeymoon with God. It is a process of self-emptying. It is a growth in consciousness of God's loving concern for us. The result of this "mystical union" with God's uncreated energies immanently living within us and loving us is that we are impelled to love God in return with a similar self-giving.

Love is always paradoxically measured by the degree of emptiness to which we are ready to submit on behalf of the beloved. We are not, in true love, looking for a reward. We do not even seek God as a separated object given to us because we have done something. An inner compulsion, nothing less than God's own love in us, His uncreated energies of the Father, Son and Holy Spirit, pushes us to new heights of letting go in self-surrender to God.

The higher levels of the mystical life touch the process of man being pushed by God's grace, His loving activity as indwelling, to take his conscious knowledge of himself, of God and of the world and to bring it into the dark regions of the unexplored unconscious. In the absence of any sensible signs of God's presence and love through consolation or images, the contemplative Christian yields the control over his life into God's loving care. It is the handmaid of the Lord in her lowliness being lovingly regarded by God. In her emptiness the Mary in all of us is being filled.

NESTING IN THE ROCK

The word *nesting* was chosen to highlight the continued, active and creative response of man to build the nest. Each nest is an intricate construction, an amazing fabrication of a bird following its God-given instincts as to how to build the shelter for new life. God also moves the bird to select the place of most security: in a rock, a high and sturdy branch, a crotch in a tree.

We have lost, through sin, the ability to "tune" in with God's communication. The first man and woman are described as communing with God but when they sinned against God's commands, they hid from Yahweh among the trees of the garden (Gn 3:8). God's continued giving of Himself to man through His Word, spoken in man's heart and listened to by man in loving acceptance was rejected by sin. God is always present, speaking His loving Word. Yet we are not always *present* to Him. We run and hide from His loving presence (Gn 3:10).

We are made "according to God's Image" that is Jesus Christ. The Risen Jesus is shining *diaphanously* through each event but we sit in darkness. He walks in our streets and wants to be "eastered" by us, to be recognized in breaking bread with the poor and oppressed. But we fear to let go and "see" Him in the present moment. In our insecurity and isolation we build bigger walls, talk compulsively of our own attainments, tear others down by aggressive attacks upon them in word, thought or deed. Or we simply withdraw from them in "splendid isolation" and gross self-righteousness.

Jesus has come among us, gentle and humble, and has given Himself to us in total emptying of Himself for us on the Cross. He has imaged for us the length, the breadth, the height and the depth of the love of God the Father for us. He pours out His Spirit so that we may see that same loving presence pouring itself out in each event that surrounds us and breaks upon us at every moment.

Yet we fail to see, to "come into" each event and there discover God's call to build our nest in Him, our Rock. He calls us to believe in His infinite love. He begs us to trust in

His faithful love in what will happen. Above all, He calls us into a spiritual childhood that progressively becomes realized as we lovingly abandon our lives to His guidance.

He is God and therefore He can, in justice, do with us whatever He wishes. That is called resignation and obedience to His holy will as manifested by His commands. But the Holy Spirit reveals in deeper prayer, in the depths of our consciousness, healed by the loving presence of Jesus, the Divine Physician, that God is our tender, loving Father. He is always acting at all times. But the Spirit convinces us by giving us new "eyes" to see that He acts always out of love for us. Our Father is always loving us.

You may reach this conclusion by way of a head-trip, a logical deduction from the fact that God's essence is love and He cannot act against His nature. But only the Spirit of Jesus can bring this into our hearts and make this truth a transforming, operative reality in each moment. ". . . because the love of God has been poured into our hearts by the Holy Spirit which has been given us (Rm 5:5).

The building of the nest in the Rock that is Jesus Christ, the Image of the Father, takes place in your material existence, in this *now* moment. "Well, now is the favorable time, this is the day of salvation" (2 Co 6:2). The past and future meet in this event that calls you to enter it with hope but, above all, with loving abandonment to the Trinity that is present in its dynamic, loving creative energies.

God loves you infinitely. He already sees you as beautiful, His noble child. Jesus has already made it possible that you are, through His Spirit dwelling in you, a child of God (Rm 8:15; Ga 4:6). "Think of the love that the Father has lavished on us, by letting us be called God's children" (1 Jn 3:1). But why don't you see what you really are? When will you give up your insecurities that you mistakenly think are your true strength?

Contemplation is God's freeing of us from our false selves. It is a long process. But it is always beginning with the event of *this* moment. There God is incarnating His loving Word again, but now in your present life, not in Bethlehem. In this present now of your life, Jesus is dying and rising and He calls you to enter into the same process.

> 'If anyone wants to be a follower of mine, let him renounce himself and take up his cross and follow me. For anyone who wants to save his life will lose it; but anyone who loses his life for my sake will find it' (Mt 16:24-25).

But it is not merely a process of suffering the cross. Abandonment is the greatest creative openness of the Christian to experience, even now within the darkness of letting go and entering into the void, the in-filling of the Risen Lord, raising His follower to a new level of union with Him. "Was it not ordained that the Christ should suffer and so enter into his glory?" (Lk 24:26).

This moment is a call to resurrection! I write these lines on Easter Day. May the Risen Jesus raise you from moment to moment, in each event to "see" your loving Father calling you to build your nest in Him, your immovable Rock. May you bring forth by the power of the Holy Spirit who hovers with His mighty pinions over you, as you build your nest, much new life. May each moment be a symbol of the nest where you are both brought to new life and where you become a channel to bring new life into this world by the love of the Spirit.

George A. Maloney, S.J.
Easter, 1977

1

From Absence to Presence

One of the most enslaving and crippling moods that can come over you and me is the fear of being alone. Basically we are afraid of not being loved, not wanted by others or by another. We fear isolation because God made us to be "toward" others. In such love relationships we come alive to our true selves. We "know" who we are in the call given to us by "another" to come and be one with that loving, caring person.

If that fear becomes actualized and we find ourselves isolated from friends, thrown into a land of strangers who treat us as a mere "thing," a terrifying, de-humanizing process begins to eat away at our interior. We move inside of our mind through crooked roads, covered with black fog. We enter a cemetery of upturned tombstones. Cut off from our true selves, we imagine sinister beasts and spirits hedging us in. False images and idols are created. Fear builds an unreal world from which we feel incapable of escaping. Who shall deliver us from such false idols? The Prophet Jeremiah speaks:

. . . every goldsmith blushes for the idol he has made, since his images are nothing but delusion, with no breath in them. They are a Nothing, a laughable production; when the time comes for them to be punished, they will vanish. (Jr 10:14-15)

ESCAPE INTO NOISE

The common way of escaping such gnawing loneliness is to surround ourselves with movement, activities, noises. The electronic age of TV and transitors has made it possible to be constantly immersed in noise. Housewives do their cooking and house-cleaning with a constant drone of TV commercials in the background. Students, fearing to concentrate in solitude, need high decibel rock music to put them into a mood.

Even our retreat houses offer a wide variety of books, tapes, lectures, discussions and group dynamics to keep restaurants busy and not bored with their solitude. But all such activities can serve to distract us for a time only and the confrontation with our deeper selves still awaits us. Carl G. Jung writes about the courage it takes to confront the hidden areas of ourselves that we cleverly cover over by masks:

True, whoever looks into the mirror of the water will see first of all his own face. Whoever goes to himself risks a confrontation with himself. The mirror does not flatter, it faithfully shows whatever looks into it; namely, the face we never show to the world because we cover it with the *persona*, the mask of the actor. But the mirror lies behind the mask and shows the true face.

This confrontation is the first test of courage on the inner way, a test sufficient to frighten off most people, for the meeting with ourselves belongs to the more unpleasant things that can be avoided so long as we can project everything negative into the environment. But if we are able to see our own shadow and can bear knowing about it, then a small part of the problem has already been solved: we have at least brought up the personal unconscious. [1]

The dark side of our inner self is threatening to our habitual control exercised over ourselves. We will do almost anything to avoid entering into the cave of our heart to do battle with the demonic forces found there. We pathetically think we have silenced the clamoring voices from deep down only to find them screaming their strident revenge in unconscious projections that we hurl at the passing world around us.

Jesus taught the necessity of letting the seed fall into the dark earth and there die, but all in order that greater fruit would result (Jn 12:24). We resist this dying process. We have an anxious dread of it. But until we let go in perfect surrender to God's indwelling Spirit, we will always be in bondage to the dark forces within us.

Thomas Merton comments on the need to pass through such fear in order to surrender more completely to Christ:

Now we can understand that full maturity of spiritual life cannot be reached unless we first pass through dread, anguish, trouble, and fear that necessarily accompany the inner crises of spiritual death in which we finally abandon our attachment to our exterior self and surrender ourselves completely to Christ. But when this surrender has been truly made, there is no longer place for fear and dread, no doubt or hesitation in the mind of one who is completely and finally resolved to seek nothing and do nothing but what is willed by Him, by God's love. [2]

A HEALING SOLITUDE

The first step to a healing comes when we can enter sincerely into our brokenness and sinfulness and recognize the urgency to receive healing. As the Spirit of God lets His light of truth shine upon our true selves, we become filled with a sense of our nothingness and sinfulness before the All-Holy God and there is a breaking in our spirit. Our props and pretty speeches fall flat. We stand impotent before God, empty before His richness, a beggar with nothing to give. "My sacrifice is this broken spirit. You will not scorn this crushed and broken heart" (Ps 51:17). God is free to do with us what He wants. True inner silence is now manifested as poverty of spirit. God must take the initiative to show us His face. We can only wait for Him to speak His reconciling word of forgiveness and healing. "Speak, Yahweh, Your servant is listening" (1S 3:9), "Let what you have said be done to me" (Lk 1:38).

Alone in the interior sanctuary desecrated by sin, I become aware that living in selfishness disintegrates and separates me from God, my true self and my outer community. Thus going down into such solitude is not an exercise in egoism but is the first step to true spiritual regeneration. In discovering myself as separated from God, my Center, and also from others, I touch the sensitive nerve of my interior fears and anguish: the separation from my true self.

Evagrius of the Egyptian desert of the fourth century knew that he left men in order to find them. A new sense of community is experienced when we, in solitude from others and in the healing presence of God, can confess our brokenness and isolation from God and fellowmen. Such solitude is healing and the necessary stage of a greater responsibility to the human race. Merton describes the paradox of being alone in solitude to find a new oneness with all human beings:

> . . . it is in fact the function of solitude to make one realize such things with a clarity that would be impossible to anyone completely immersed in the other cares, the other illusions, and all the automatisms of a tightly collective existence . . . It is because I am one with them that I owe it to them to be alone, and when I am alone they are not "they" but my own self. There are no strangers.[3]

THE COURAGE TO BELIEVE

It takes courage to confront the fear of being alone. To avow that we have turned away from love toward self-absorption is to begin an advance toward true human freedom and love. This is somewhat the negative side of true, healing solitude: recognizing our failures to love as we should have. But such penitence leads us in faith to the healing presence of God. We cry out for mercy, knowing now in a total experience of inner poverty that we cannot heal ourselves.

It takes greater courage in solitude to take the next step: to enter into the loving presence of God and to believe with total commitment that God will be faithful to us. This was the courage in solitude that Abraham, Moses and Elijah showed in their total surrender to serve God.

The *Book of Hebrews* holds up Abraham especially as the father of faith. "It was through his faith that Abraham obeyed the call to set out for a country that was the inheritance . . . without knowing where he was going" (Heb 11:8). In the case of Abraham, as William of St.

Thierry points out,[4] his faith was an interpersonal relationship between God and him. God had promised to be faithful to Abraham, a "Thou's Self-acrediting, a Self-commitment" to him. He had no idea how God intended in the face of such a contradiction to keep His promise if Abraham sacrificed his only son. Yet he believed that somehow, beyond his own reasoning power, God would be true to His commitment.

Abraham responds with a similar absolute fidelity to God. He finds his transcendent, true self in the certitude of his faith in God. God is his absolute Center. He is free to ask Abraham anything. Abraham gives up his control over his life and paradoxically finds his full life in his fidelity to God.

ABANDONMENT TO GOD IS TO LET GO

Essential to faith similar to that of Abraham that we as Christians are enjoined to possess if we are to be justified is an interior experience of God's presence as a *Thou.* If I am to move away from anonymity and meaningless isolation, away from absence of an ultimate Center, I must enter into a dialectical movement toward God as a *presenced* Center. This cannot be reasoned to by my own intellectual powers. I can only humbly cry out for such a loving presence to come to me in my need.

> In your loving kindness, answer me, Yahweh,
> in your great tenderness turn to me;
> do not hide your face from your servant,
> quick, I am in trouble, answer me;
> come to my side, redeem me,
> from so many enemies ransom me (Ps 69: 16-18).

Such faith is a graceful gift of God's personal presence to the broken, little ones of His Kingdom. He condescends to come to their side to help them. He pledges His unconditional word that He will be faithful. "Always true to his promises, Yahweh shows love in all he does" (Ps 145:13).

When we are given such a gift of God's presence as dynamically loving us in every event and moment, then complete *abandonment* is our true response to His fidelity to us. There is no longer any solitude. God is ever at our side. We are freed at last from our greatest fear of being alone, that no one will care for us. "With God on our side who can be against us?" (Rm 8:31).

St. Paul, like the early Christians, had experienced faith, not as an intellectual assent to a given revealed truth but as an I-Thou relationship of God's loving presence acting out His fidelity in all circumstances of Paul's life. He singles out his response to God's fidelity. No trouble, no worry, no persecution, no lack of food or clothing, no threats or attacks could ever take him away from the love of Christ.

For I am certain of this: neither death nor life, no angel, no prince, nothing that exists, nothing still to come, not any power, or height or depth, nor any created thing, can ever come between us and the love of God made visible in Christ Jesus our Lord (Rm 8:38-39).

CHILDREN OF GOD

This abandonment or letting go on our part flows from the faith that God's Holy Spirit infuses into us. In this gift we experience that we are loved absolutely and eternally by

God, our loving Father. The Spirit of Jesus is sent into our hearts (Rm 5:5) and dwells there (Rm 8:9), giving us the experience that we are *truly* His children and we can call Him by the endearing, affectionate title of *Abba,* Father (Rm 8:15; Ga 4:6).

This faith credits God with omnipotence — that all things in the whole world, every atom, every event, great and small — all are under His guiding power. But it goes beyond that. It credits God with being *my* Father. He loves me more tenderly, with greater constancy and concern, than any human being ever could. He is love and all His actions are directed out of His fatherly love for His children.

I belong to God, my Father, because He has created me and continues to preserve me in existence. But God is uniquely my Father and yours because He has created us "according to His Image" (Gn 1:26), that is Jesus Christ (Col 1:15). God has so loved us as to give us His only begotten Son so that whoever believes in Him will have eternal life (Jn 3:16). We are made truly His children by adoption through His Holy Spirit.

> The proof that you are sons is that God has sent the Spirit of his Son into our hearts: the Spirit that cries, 'Abba, Father,' and it is this that makes you a son. You are not a slave any more, and if God has made you a son, then he has made you heir (Ga 4:6-7).

We are made participators of His very nature, by grace (2 P 1:14). We are born from above, by the power of God, to become children of God (Jn 1:12) by His will through Christ Jesus. This regeneration is brought about by the Spirit (Jn 3:8) who dwells within us, making our bodies true temples of God (1 Co 3:16; 6:19).

THE TRANSFORMING HOLY SPIRIT

The redemptive work of Jesus Christ can be seen as an "unconcealment" of this awesome presence of the indwelling Trinity, Father, Son and Holy Spirit, but as creative fidelity in love to bring us ever more present in consciousness to this great love and thus surrender ourselves to become in the process loving children. This is a state of highest expanded consciousness brought about by an increased infusion of faith, hope and love by the Holy Spirit. It is only the Spirit who assures us that we are united with God and truly growing in greater loving union. He gives us the courage and faith to surrender to God's love in all circumstances and thus progressively become more and more His loving children.

Now in abandoning ourselves to God's loving presence in each moment, we are able to pray incessantly because it is truly the power of the Spirit that prays within us, as St. Paul says:

> . . . the Spirit himself expresses our plea in a way that could never be put into words, and God who knows everything in our hearts knows perfectly well what he means . . . (Rm 8:27).

The Spirit allows us to let go of our preconceived ideas of reality, of what we deem to be important and not so important. He gives us a whole new set of values that are truly illogical to the wordly-minded (1 Co 1:18), that only

the little children of the Kingdom of Heaven can understand because:

> These are the very things that God has revealed to us
> through the Spirit, for the Spirit reaches the depths of
> everything, even the depths of God . . . the depths of God
> can only be known by the Spirit of God . . . we have
> received the Spirit that comes from God, to teach us to
> understand the gifts that he has given us (1 Co 2:10-12).

The progress in our spiritual transformation by the
Holy Spirit into loving children of God in union with Jesus
Christ, the first-born of the Father, is measured by the
degree of surrender we make of our whole lives to the
Father. No longer do we "strive for perfection." We relax
and let go, yielding to the power of God's Spirit to effect
what is impossible to us. We silence our dispersion out-
wardly towards the possession of things. We move into a
state of habitual prayer of listening to the Father bring
forth His word within us, ever so gently, ever so gradually,
but always in the context of our daily lives and the events
that make them up.

Recollection or the inward silence of our hearts is
striving for that "still point" of attentiveness so that God
may speak His word whenever and however He wishes. The
Spirit pushes our consciousness down through various
levels of knowledge until we sink into the "cloud of
unknowing," the state of surrendering our controlled
knowledge of God and of ourselves and of the world to a
new knowledge that only the Spirit of God will infuse as a
gift. He taps into the regions beneath the habitual surface
of our existence that we learn to turn over to God's healing
love and control.

The seeds of tremendous potentiality lie in that dark womb but only for those who have the courage to live in the dark mystery of God's loving presence that is seen by not seeing "with a loving, striving, blindly beholding the naked being only of God Himself" (*The Cloud of Unknowing*). Abandoned to God's loving fidelity, His creative activity to bring us into "the utter fullness of God," we can learn to let go more and more of the areas of our lives held in control by our own power and isolation from God.

Paradoxically we experience that God does not abandon us but we only then find Him as our loving Father and we realize with immense joy our true identity as His loving children. It is in the darkness of our creaturely poverty and sterility that we allow God to perform a new work of transforming us into new creatures in Christ Jesus. Solitude and poverty become community and the inheritance of Heaven with Christ forever.

Abandoning ourselves to God's love is to find ourselves in the true knowledge that is beyond our own striving. It is a gift given to God's chosen little ones. Let us pray for this precious gift without which we cannot be our true selves, in the words of St. Paul:

> Out of his infinite glory, may he give you the power through his Spirit for your hidden self to grow strong, so that Christ may live in your hearts through faith, and then, planted in love and built on love, you will with all the saints have strength to grasp the breadth and the length, the height and the depth; until, knowing the love of Christ which is beyond all knowledge, you are filled with the utter fullness of God (Ep 3:16-19).

"THE FATHER HIMSELF LOVES YOU" [Jn 16:27]

A strange phenomenon occurs in the spiritual lives of most of us. Although our Heavenly Father is the source of our being, He who first loved us (1 Jn 4:19), nevertheless for most of us it takes many years of Christian living before we enter into a deep, loving relationship with our Father in Heaven. Perhaps one reason for this is that no matter how good our earthly father was, we need to work out the limitations that we have thus experienced of fatherhood.

But perhaps the most important reason for a delayed devotion to God the Father is that it takes quite a bit of human living to let go of our lives in trusting love toward another person. Sin in our members fills us with a fear of letting go and loving others. We are blessed if we, as children, have experienced deep love from a father, mother, brothers and sisters and friends. That is usually a sheer gift, undeserved on our part, given because of the goodness of those around us who offer us their love, often of an instinctual nature through blood relationships.

Do you remember, however, the first time you encountered love from "outside" the blood line? Didn't you stop and wonder why he or she should love you? The love from family ties was rather implicitly taken for granted. It was there as long as you could remember. But why was this "outsider" loving you? There was something different to this love. It was *free*. He or she apparently wanted to give you love. And you knew you had nothing to return — except yourself. Ah, that was what made this love so exciting. You were being loved for yourself! You possessed some nobility and beauty that attracted the other person to love you.

As we experience such gratuitous love, freely given, it becomes easier to let go and believe that even God could love us freely. But I believe that is why the love of our Heavenly Father becomes a real experience for most of us only after many years of human living and loving. It takes so long to experience true human love and to believe in it so as to return freely that love offered. We receive love and enjoy it, but we continuously doubt that love. After years of marriage the wife startles the husband with her question: "Do you *really* love me?"

GOD LOVES US

We might try as a philosopher to reason that God loves us because He could only act out of His own perfection whose essence is love or self-giving, but we would always doubt His love. Because God has so loved us, however, as to give us Jesus (Jn 3:16), we now have the *Way*, the *Truth* and the *Life* that leads us to the loving Father. The redemptive power of Jesus consists in sending us His Holy Spirit who progressively teaches us in our daily life that God the Father loves us infinitely in Christ Jesus.

God's love for us was revealed
when God sent into the world his only Son
so that we could have life through him;
this is the love I mean:
not our love for God,
but God's love for us when he sent his Son
to be the sacrifice that takes our sins away (1 Jn 4:9-10).

Jesus is the perfect Image of the Heavenly Father (Col 1:15). The Spirit allows us to see the Father in Him.

No one can come to the Father except through me.
If you know me, you know my Father too.
. . . To have seen me is to have seen the Father (Jn 14:6-9).

Jesus came to reveal to us that we have a loving Father. He came as part of being God's "unconcealing" Word to act out in human language of suffering love unto death the immense love of the Father for us. As we contemplate Jesus stripped on the Cross, emptied of His very life, which is poured out until the last drop of blood and water (Jn 19:34), the Holy Spirit reveals to us how the Father has spoken all of His love for us in His single Word. God reaches a limit in human communication of His love for us human beings. For what can God or man do more to prove love than to suffer freely unto death for the one loved? "A man can have no greater love than to lay down his life for his friends" (Jn 15:13).

We are healed by His wounds (Is 53:5) only to the degree that the Spirit of Jesus convinces us in prayer that all this suffering is freely being done for us to reveal that this is how much our Heavenly Father loves us. We are justified when we live in faith given us by the Holy Spirit, "faith in the Son of God who loved me and who sacrificed himself for my sake" (Ga 2:20).

As we experience in our spiritual life that Jesus freely dies in an eternal *now* for us individually, we gradually become convinced that He is imagining the Father's love. "I have made your name known to them and will continue to make it known, so that the love with which you loved me may be in them, and so that I may be in them" (Jn 17:26).

THE FATHER INDWELLS

We can believe "in God the Father almighty, Creator of heaven and earth." We can believe God has poured out His love in the millions of gifts that He lavishes upon us. All the beautiful creatures that God gives to us cry out as signposts pointing to our great Benefactor. The variety of beauty in His gifts, the richness, the plenitude that we have all received leave us breathless before God's generosity. St. Augustine cries out:

> Heaven and earth and all that is in the universe cry out to me from all directions that I, O God, must love Thee, and they do not cease to cry out to all so that they have no excuse.

But God's love is a self-giving that seeks to be a constant presence of fidelity. Not only is He present in His gifts, but He seeks to share His very *being* with us. At times we catch glimpses of His burning love. When in prayer we understand that God seeks to be so present to us that He lives within us, His total being, in His uncreated energies, surrounds us, possesses us, lives immanently within us. Praise God for His love that places God within us in a state of constant self-giving to us. Truly we marvel to think of God's condescending love for us.

> Ah, what is man that you should spare a thought for him,
> the son of man that you should care for him?
> Yet you have made him little less than a god,
> you have crowned him with glory and splendour . . . (Ps 8:4-5).

By faith we can believe the Good News that Jesus makes possible by His Holy Spirit: ". . . and my Father will love him, and we shall come to him and make our home with him" (Jn 14:23). If the Father dwells in us He loves us in Jesus. In His Spirit of love He begets us into the likeness of His beloved Son Jesus. He does not call us His children in any extrinsic fashion. But He transforms us into new creatures in Christ Jesus (2 Co 5:17). This is the mystery that amazes St. John the Evangelist as he writes:

> Think of the love that the Father has lavished on us,
> by letting us be called God's children;
> and that is what we are.
> . . . My dear people, we are already the children of God
> but what we are to be in the future
> has not yet been revealed . . . (1 Jn 3:1-2).

Mystics throughout the centuries have experienced this "immersion" into God and have shared with us what it meant to them. We can have momentary flashes of God's nearness, even inter-penetration within our very being. But these flashes only leave us in greater aweful amazement at God's humble love shown towards us.

One of the great Byzantine mystics, St. Symeon the

New Theologian (+ 1022) allows us to ponder what the divine indwelling meant to him:

> Indeed, it is an awesome thing,
> Master, awesome even beyond any word,
> that I see the light that the world does not possess,
> that He loves me who is not within this world,
> and that I love Him who has no part with visible things.
> I am seated on my couch completely lost to the world.
> And, being in the middle of my cell, I see Him
> who is outside of the world as here present,
> I see Him and I converse with Him
> and, dare I then to say it!
> I love Him and He loves me.
> I eat, I nourish myself with only this contemplation.
> And being made one with Him, I am transported above to the heavens.
> That this is true and certain I know,
> but where then is my body, this I do not know.
> I know that He who remains immovable descends.
> I know that He who is invisible appears to me.
> I know that He who is separated from all creation
> takes me within Himself and hides me in His arms.
> And I am completely outside of the whole world.
> But I, so mortal, so insignificant in the world, contemplate in myself
> completely the Creator of the world.
> And I know that I will not die
> because I am inside of life,
> and that I have the entire life that completely flows out from within me.
> He is in my heart
> He dwells in Heaven;
> both here and there He is seen by me equally dazzling. [1]

IN THE BOSOM OF THE FATHER

One of the most beautiful descriptions of Jesus' relationship to His Heavenly Father is given in St. John's Prologue: "No one has ever seen God; it is the only Son, who is nearest to the Father's heart, who has made him known" (Jn 1:18). The phrase "nearest to the Father's heart (or bosom) is rendered in Latin by the phrase, "in sinu Patris." John the Beloved disciple leaned on the *bosom* of Jesus (Jn 13:23). In Scripture *in sinu* has deep meanings.

William of St. Thierry gives us an important nuance of what constitutes a *person* through love relationships. He coins the word, *insinuatio,* to describe that the Son and the Father are two lovers, not at arms length, but they take each other to their breasts in an embrace. They give themselves to each other by "uncovering" themselves to each other and they mutually allow each other to known his identity in that mutual uncovering. Jesus knows the mind of the Father and reveals it to all who open to His revelation.

Jesus finds His whole *person* in being the total narration, unconcealment and manifestation of the Other, His Father. To know Him then is to know the Other. Their mutual embrace, interpenetration and unconcealment is so much as one through love for each other that one cannot be separated from the Other. It would follow then that our immersion with Jesus and the Father would make us an "unconcealment" of them to all we meet. Here are William's words:

> In effect, no one has ever seen God with these bodily eyes; but since the only Son is the very insinuation of the Father (in sinu Patris), and thereby uncovers the Father in an unspeakable telling, the purified and holy rational creature

is permeated with this inexpressible vision. The creature is able to understand the Speaker narrating because He is *logos*—not the kind of word that strikes the ear as sound, but rather something like an *imago* disclosed to the spirit. By an interior and manifest light this telling clarifies the words of the Lord: "Philip, whoever sees me sees the Father too."[2]

The exciting revelation that Jesus comes to give us and, through His Holy Spirit, to effect in us is that the Father loves us as Jesus Himself loves us. Jesus is the one "nearest to the Father's heart." He unconceals the depths of the Father's love for us. As we experience the burning love that the Father has for us individually, we become like to Jesus, the Image of the Father. Like Jesus we can surrender to the Father's love in all moments of our lives. Love begets love. The Father's love experienced begets loving children who are one with His only begotten Son, Jesus.

Yet how can we comprehend the love of the Father imaged in the love of Jesus for us? That is St. Paul's prayer to the Father that the Christians of Ephesus may comprehend the breadth and length and height and depth, to know Christ's love which surpasses all human knowledge (Ep 3:18-19). Our abandonment to our Heavenly Father follows according to the love of the Father that we experience in the imaged love of Jesus for us. We turn to Jesus to see how He abandoned Himself to His Father.

3

The Abandonment of Jesus to The Father

If our Heavenly Father loves us with such an infinite love as imaged by the emptied Jesus on the Cross, how much more does Jesus experience the fullness of the Father's love for Him personally! How perfectly does Jesus, always and not merely in His earthly existence, abandon Himself in love to His Father!

In our limited experiences we are aware that our potential to return love is measured by the degree of love received. Are the juvenile delinquents in our courts, in our correction institutions, on our streets spewing out hatred and violent crimes often toward the elderly and the defenseless not proof that all of us are the result of love received or the lack of such love. Loving people call us into a transcendence of self-giving in return. With no love received, we resort to violence to shout out in defiance to the world that we deserve to be loved.

No human consciousness ever grew progressively in receiving love from the all-holy Heavenly Father as did Jesus. At every moment He was aware of this perfect love pouring into Him and calling Him to a similar response.

How explicitly Jesus reveals to us in the Last Supper Discourse this love that He had received from His Father during His whole lifetime.

As the Father has loved me,
so I have loved you. . . .
just as I have kept my Father's commandments
and remain in his love (Jn 15:9-10).

---the world will realize that it was you who sent me
and that I have loved them as much as you loved me (Jn 17:23).

Over the long years of intimacy in the silence of Nazareth this love of the Father poured into Jesus, calling Him to a like response of love, filling Him with an awesome reverence for His Father and a perfect humility that recognized the Father as the Source of His whole being. Under the stars, praying at night during His public ministry, Jesus touched the heart of His loving Father and gained new power to love the broken people who would come to Him the next day for healing, to receive the Word of eternal life.

THE HUMILITY OF JESUS

In experiencing the Father's great love, Jesus experienced the truth that everything came to Him from the Father. He realized clearly that He could do nothing by Himself without the Father (Jn 5:19,30). "My teaching is not from myself; it comes from the one who sent me" (Jn 7:16; Jn 8:28).

Jesus seeks not His own glory.

Not that I care for my own glory,
There is someone who takes care of that
and is the judge of it (Jn 8:50).

    The magnificent obsession in the life of Jesus was centered around doing only His Father's will. As Jesus taught us in the Lord's Prayer, so He lived. "Your will be done, on earth as in heaven" (Mt 6:10). He was about His Father's business (Lk 2:49). St. Paul writes: "Christ did not think of himself" (Rm 15:3). He only sought always to "do what pleases him (His Father)" (Jn 8:29).

My food
is to do the will of the one who sent me,
and to complete his work (Jn 4:34).

    Jesus could appeal to His gentleness and humility to be imitated by us because He was essentially gentle and humble before His Father (Mt 11:30). He could afford to be so before His Father and before all human beings who met Him because He was constantly living in the loving presence of His Father who sustained Him in His being. The Father poured out His creative loving energies endlessly. Jesus was merely the Word that received His total meaning—fulness from the eternal Mind that spoke the Word.
    In each event of every moment Jesus experienced the dynamic, active love of the Father working in Him and in all of nature around Him. "My Father goes on working and so do I" (Jn 5:17). Jesus freely consents to work according to His Father's holy will. His total sufficiency came from God His Father (2 Co 3:5). He could cast all care on Him who cared for Him (1 P 5:7).

ONE IN HIM

Jesus was able to surrender Himself to the loving presence of His Father in each event because He had learned to find that same Father working deeply within Him, in His "heart," in the deepest reaches of His consciousness. It was there in the depths of His being, in His core or at His center that He contemplated the Father as loving Him and begetting Him into His image. As Jesus let go of His life in loving submission to the Father loving Him in total self-giving, He grew in the consciousness that He spoke of in His prayer to the Father:

Father, may they be one in us,
as you are in me and I am in you,
so that the world may believe it was you who sent me.
I have given them the glory you gave to me,
that they may be one as we are one.
With me in them and you in me
may they be so completely one
that the world will realize that it was you who sent me
and that I have loved them as much as you loved me (Jn 17:21-23).

As Jesus prayerfully allowed the Father's love to enter into all levels of His consciousness and unconscious, much as the story of His temptations in the desert shows, He learned to let go of the control He exercised over His own human existence. He experienced at one and the same time the immense love of the Father and the ontological necessity of returning that love in an abandonment that would lead eventually to His ignominious death on the Cross. Especially in the agony of Gethsemane and on the

Cross, Jesus entered into the black darkness of His inner self and there struggled with the test of identity. Was He to worship the Lord God and serve Him alone (Dt 6:13; Mt 4:10) or was He to yield to fear and doubt and grasp in self-centeredness to hold on to His life?

DARK ABANDONMENT

In the Garden heaviness, fright, sorrow, disgust and loathing comes over Him. Fear, a new experience for Jesus, comes over Him and He wants to run away from it all. He prays a real wish: "Father, if you are willing, take this cup away from me" (Lk 22:42). His sweat fell to the ground like great drops of blood. What a tremendous burst of love is generated in Jesus' soul as He returns the Father's great love over all His lifetime in the burst of self-abandonment: "nevertheless, let your will be done, not mine" (Lk 22:43).

Love that generates into abandonment in the heart of Jesus admits of varying degrees of surrendering to the Father's love. In the temptations in the desert and in Gethsemane, Jesus struggles to embrace the holy will of the Father which is demanding complete obedience to Him. He proved Himself submissive and obedient to what His consciousness at the time reveals to be the Father's expressed command. "Here I am! I am coming to obey your will" (Heb 10:9).

But on the Cross, unlike the desert and garden experience where Jesus was comforted by an angel, Jesus freely enters into the deepest levels of abandonment. In the greatest temptation on the Cross, the final degree of abandonment to the Father's love, Jesus begins to feel the awful absence of the Father's love.

Nowhere does the light of the Father's warm love for

Jesus, His beloved Son, appear. There is only black darkness, chilling doubt. Was He mistaken over all those years that His Father really loved Him? Was He really His only begotten Son? Where is His Father? "If You love me, show Your face! What have I done to deserve Your anger? Didn't I always do Your will? Why do You treat me like this?"

Swirling black clouds of despair rise up. A cry of anguish, "My God, my God, why have You deserted me?" (Mk 15:24). Groping for a shred of light, Jesus surrenders Himself totally to the Father. He lets go the last hold on His existence. He always sought to please His Father. Now Jesus returns His life to the Father with nothing in return of experienced love and His Father's good pleasure.

"Father, into your hands I commit my spirit" (Lk 23:46). Jesus passes over in His *exodus* into a blind abandonment into His Father's hands, who is now free to do with Him whatever He wishes.

Jesus, obedient unto death (Ph 2:8), reaches a oneness with the Father never before experienced in His human consciousness. The Father glorifies Him as His true Son, the perfect Image of the Father's love for mankind.

LOVE, THE MEASURE OF ABANDONMENT

Jesus teaches us that abandonment is not a static resignation of Himself to His Father's will. Love for another is a continued process of surrendering oneself to that person in a desire to become more totally *one* with that person. To love is to surrender to the good pleasure of the other.

To the degree that Jesus experiences His Father's love for Him, to that degree He strives in greater spontaneity and inner freedom to return His love to the Father. Abandonment becomes an inventive process whereby Jesus is interiorly prompted to give, in each moment, more and more of His consciousness over to His Father. The Heavenly Father had poured the fullness of His divinity into Jesus (Col 2:9). He held back nothing of Himself in His perfect love given His only begotten Son through His Spirit.

The power of love is that it creates in the one loved a passionate desire to become like the lover. Like attracts like by a union that dissolves separation and anonymity and makes the two into one being. The community established in unity calls out, however, the uniqueness of each person. Freedom experienced in self-surrender leads to a new awareness of an identity through loving acceptance of *me* as a person lovable.

In the continued experiences that Jesus had during His human existence on earth of His Father's infinite love for Him, there grew to an ever-greater swelling, like a cascading mountain stream gaining momentum and power as it approaches closer to the sea, His desire to be loving like His Father. Jesus' abandonment goes beyond seeking to do the commands of His Father.

Can we not find a fuller understanding of what abandonment as a return of love meant to Jesus in a theological insight at the heart of the mystery of the Incarnation? Jesus, as the incarnate Word, finds His mission in becoming the full expression of God's love for us. Jesus progressively, as He experiences the Father's love for Him, seeks to express in human choices that love. "As the Father has loved me, so I have loved you" (Jn 15:9).

It is especially when His hour was approaching, in which Jesus would definitively speak as God's spoken Word of the immense love of God for us, that Jesus reaches a peak of abandonment. He pushes Himself to new heights of creative surrender to His Father. He wants, eagerly desires, to partake of this baptism of the Spirit of love, to be poured out as molten wax. He wishes to be dissolved of all self-containment in order to be united in complete oneness in love with His Father.

No longer is there a mere seeking to obey the Father's commands or expressed desires. Jesus burns freely to choose the best way to equalize the love He has so abundantly received from the Father. All his lifetime He sought to do what would most please His Father. "For I do always those things that please Him" (Jn 8:29). But in His passion, in the excruciating interior humiliations and utter abandonment by His Father, Jesus freely goes forth and desires to empty Himself. "More darkness, more emptiness" could be His cry as Jesus moves into the full expression of God's love for mankind.

Such abandonment can only be experienced in a state of similar love received and given as Jesus had experienced. The Spirit of Jesus alone will reveal to us all about Jesus (Jn 14:26). He alone will reveal to us the infinite love of Jesus as the expressed Image of the Heavenly Father. He alone will lead us into an abandonment that will be in proportion to the great love that the Father, Abba, has for each of us. We will begin to be Christians when the love of the Father experienced in our hearts through the outpouring of the Holy Spirit will be freely acted out by a progressively free desire to abandon ourselves totally to the Father in all things.

4

Be Not Anxious

Christianity is a *prophetic* religion. God communicates Himself to mankind by speaking His Word. He is made a loving presence to us in His living Word. God's prophetic Word in Holy Scripture reveals to us objective reality, concrete ideas about God's true nature, our own ultimate destiny and the means we are to use to attain our fulfillment. But God's Word releases an inner dynamism, a creative power of transforming love within the hearts of those who prayerfully hear that Word.

We find this exemplified in the Old Testament. God's Word is a dynamic force in which God creates the world as a sign of His ardent desire to share Himself with men and He effects the sign by actually communicating Himself in His creative Word (Ps 33: 4-9). God is an energy within man, creating him marvelously, knowing all his thoughts and movements because His loving presence surrounds man. Man cannot escape from God's Spirit (Ps 139).

More than this, God's Word reveals Him as a God who loves man more tenderly than a mother loves her sucking child.

Does a woman forget her baby at the breast,
or fail to cherish the son of her womb?
Yet even if these forget,
I will never forget you.
See, I have branded you on the palms of my hands (Is 49:
15-16).

The Word reveals that we are not to be afraid because Yahweh has called us by our name and we belong to Him. He will protect us should we pass through the sea or rivers or through flames of fire. "Do not be afraid, for I am with you" (Is 43:5).

TRUST IN THE NEW TESTAMENT

When God's Word becomes man among us, we are taught to trust in the Heavenly Father as He, Jesus, did. But He gives us His Holy Spirit who makes it possible to abandon ourselves to our loving Father. We are to put aside all nervous and excessive anxiety about temporal concerns.

I am telling you not to worry about your life and what you are to eat, nor about your body and how you are to clothe it. For life means more than food, and the body more than clothing. Think of the ravens. They do not sow or reap; they have no storehouses and no barns; yet God feeds them. And how much more are you worth than the birds. Can any of you, for all his worrying, add a single cubit to his span of life? If the smallest things, therefore, are outside your control, why worry about the rest? . . . Now if that is how God clothes the grass, much more will he look after you, you men of little faith! But you, you must not set your hearts on things to eat and things to drink; nor must you worry. It is the pagans of this world who set their hearts on all these things. Your Father well knows you need them. No; set your

hearts on his kingdom, and these other things will be given
you as well. There is no need to be afraid, little flock, for it
has pleased your Father to give you the kingdom (Lk 12:22-
32).

Jesus teaches us that the only focus of our striving in
this earthly life must be our Heavenly Father. No person or
thing must take precedence over God in our attachment
and desige. He is not advocating a giving up of such
temporalities as food and clothing. These are important but
Jesus insists that we subordinate them always as means to
further our one end: to seek always the Kingdom of God.
He is our God and Him alone we must serve (Dt 6:13).

How truly exciting to see in our 20th century men and
women discovering this important facet of Jesus' revelation
of the Good News and then acting on it as the Word of God!
How inspiring to see a small, bent-over woman like Mother
Teresa of Calcutta, radiant with joy, as she and her sisters
go through the streets of India collecting the maimed and
the dying and believing that God will provide for all their
needs as they seek only His Kingdom. Men and women of
all backgrounds are giving up all and trusting in God's
providence to meet their needs as they seek to do His work.

Such a living out of a deep filial love and trust for our
Heavenly Father admits of many styles of life. There is not
just one way of being detached from possessions. But there
is only one way for all true Christians to live such a filial
relationship with their Father—that is, without excessive
solicitude and worry about temporalities.

SOVEREIGNTY OF GOD ALONE

The Christian concept that Jesus preached and lived of

child-like abandonment to the Heavenly Father is based on the great command to love God with our whole heart, soul and mind (Dt 6:5; Mt 22:37). St. Francis de Sales describes the love that we owe to God:

> Since God alone is Lord, since his goodness is infinitely great, infinitely above all goodness, he must be loved with a love that is nobler, stronger, more perfect than any other. This is the love that gives God the place of honor in our hearts, that makes us value so highly the blessing of being pleasing to Him, that we prefer and care for God before all things else. [1]

God alone is God. There is no god like our God. "Yahweh, you are the only one" (Ne 9:6). All creation, all life comes from Him. All authority comes from God (Rm 13:1). In HIm we live and move and have our being (Ac 17:28). Truth, therefore, demands not only that we recognize our complete dependence upon God intellectually but that in all circumstances we surrender ourselves in loving trust to His sovereignty.

WITHOUT ME YOU CAN DO NOTHING

What great wisdom to be penetrated by the Spirit's inner knowledge that we are totally weak of ourselves, but our strength is completely in God. Jesus teaches us this in His metaphor of the vine and the branches. He and the Father are one. All His power has come to Him from the Father. Thus what Jesus claims for Himself, He claims for His Father.

We must therefore abide in Him and let Him abide in us.

Make your home in me, as I make mine in you.
As a branch cannot bear fruit all by itself,
but must remain part of the vine,
neither can you unless you remain in me.
I am the vine,
you are the branches.
Whoever remains in me, with me in him,
bears fruit in plenty;
for cut off from me you can do nothing.
Anyone who does not remain in me
is like a branch that has been thrown away
—he withers (Jn 15:4-6).

The true child of God realizes in life's circumstances that he has no strength of his own. In all moments he confesses his weakness to do good for himself. He knows with St. Paul that all his strength is in Christ. True strength begins with a realized conviction that of ourselves we are weak, but our very weakness confessed becomes our strength because we lovingly surrender to God in all things (to come to our assistance.)

So I shall be very happy to make my weaknesses my special boast so that the power of Christ may stay over me, and that is why I am quite content with my weaknesses, and with insults, hardships, persecutions, and the agonies I go through for Christ's sake. For it is when I am weak that I am strong (2 Co 12:9-10).

The fruit that our Father wishes us to bring forth is a constant, loving submission and obedience to His commands and wishes. To believe that the Father truly loves us and does all things out of love is the basis for our child-like surrender. "I need only say, 'I am slipping,' and your love,

Yahweh, immediately supports me; and in the middle of all my troubles you console me and make me happy" (Ps 94:18-19). "God's decrees will never alter; holiness will distinguish your house, Yahweh, forever and ever" (Ps 93:5).

God is our Rock. Faultless are His deeds (Dt 32:4). ". . . Yahweh is righteous, my rock in whom no fault is to be found!" (Ps 92:15).

THE VINEDRESSER PRUNES

Our Heavenly Father is free, therefore, in HIs loving wisdom to prune from us whatever is not unto full life (Jn 15:1-2). He seeks only that we may receive more abundantly His divine life. The abandoned child believes in the goodness of his Father. He has learned from Jesus that, if we human beings know how to give good things to our children, how much more our Heavenly Father knows what is good and will give it (Lk 11:9-13). His faith and trust are strengthened in trials and tribulations (1 P 1:6-7) because he believes always in His Father's great love for him.

How beautifully this child-like trust in God in times of trials is brought out in the Epistle to the Hebrews that quotes from Pr 3:11-12:

> Have you forgotten that encouraging text in which you are addressed as sons? My Son, when the Lord corrects you, do not treat it lightly; but do not get discouraged when he reprimands you. For the Lord trains the ones that he loves and he punishes all those that he acknowledges as his sons. Suffering is part of your training; God is treating you as his sons. Has there ever been any son whose father did not train him? If you were not getting this training, as all of you are, then you would not be sons but bastards. Besides, we have

all had our human fathers who punished us, and we
respected them for it; we ought to be even more willing to
submit ourselves to our spiritual Father, to be given life.
Our human fathers were thinking of this short life when
they punished us, and could only do what they thought best;
but he does it all for our own good, so that we may share his
own holiness. Of course, any punishment is most painful at
the time, and far from pleasant; but later, in those on whom
it has been used, it bears fruit in peace and goodness. So
hold up your limp arms and steady your trembling knees
and smooth out the path you tread; then the injured limb
will not be wrenched, it will grow strong again (Heb 12:5-
13).

Such a child of God "puts his trust in Yahweh, with
Yahweh for his hope" (Jr 17:7) because he simply believes,
in the words of St. Paul, "that by turning everything to
their good, God cooperates with all those who love him,
with all those that he has called according to his purpose"
(Rm 8:28).

GIFT OF ONESELF

Such abandonment is the result of the Holy Spirit
making us conformed to the image of God's Son, "so that
his Son might be the eldest of many brothers" (Rm 8:29).
The Holy Spirit leads us into this childhood, giving us the
experience of being *in* Jesus, loved infinitely by our Father,
growing daily in this love. Our daily lives are grounded in
hope that gives us strength to bear sufferings with patience
and perseverance "because the love of God has been poured
into our hearts by the Holy Spirit which has been given us"
(Rm 5:4-5).

To the degree that we are guided by the Spirit, baptized in God's Spirit of love, we surrender ourselves as gift back to God who has given us everything in giving us Jesus Christ. Our gift of self to God means that every thought is brought under obedience and conformity to Jesus Christ (2 Co 10:5). We live the *Lord's Prayer* by asking that His name may be glorified in all things. But God is glorified when in all events He is loved by us. St. Augustine insisted, "God in only honored by love."[2]

Self-love is driven out of our lives by the love of God, which abounding in our hearts, allows us to live in a constant state of giving ourselves as gift to God.

We pray and by grace seek always to do His will on earth as it is done in Heaven. It is this striving to please the Father in each event that characterizes the sign of the children of Heaven. Without this childlike love there is no entrance into the Kingdom of God (Mt 18:2; Lk 18:17).

The Greek Fathers summarized all the Christian virtues into this one of childlike trust and love, called *parrhesia.* It is a progressive state infused into us by the Spirit. "The Spirit himself and our spirit bear united witness that we are children of God" (Rm 8:16). We conduct ourselves before the Father as His loving children because that is what the Spirit allows us constantly to experience. We are "heirs of God and coheirs with Christ, sharing his sufferings so as to share his glory" (Rm 8:17).

IMPORTANCE OF THE *NOW* MOMENT

For many of seeking to serve God, our values of what is important and great bespeak not a little the influence of the world. We look to do great things for God, almost implying that God has been waiting in sick bay for us to start His world moving again, that He desperately needs us and that we can do anything if we only grunt hard enough! St. Augustine called this heresy of good works without dependence on God's grace *Pelagianism*. Whatever name we give it, it is still very much with us.

Thus determining what we regard as great and waiting for such great moments to come our way, we end up very much like Vladimir and Estrogon in Samuel Beckett's play, *Waiting for Godot*. We wait for God to come in the spectacular and miss Him in the little moments of each day.

An element intrinsic to true love is constant fidelity that covers what may appear to our human eyes as great and important tasks as well as what worldlings would judge to be of little importance. Jesus had applauded such fidelity in little things in HIs parable of the talents. "Well done, good and faithful servant; you have shown you can be faithful in small things; I will trust you with greater; come and join in your master's happiness" (Mt 25:21).

We must be attentive to the distinction of littleness of mind, centered on self, fear and cowardice that are really a lack of faith, hope and love in God and littleness of value in the estimation of worldlings which can partake of greatness of mind and sublime faith, hope and love in God. Jesus lived thirty years in obscurity performing "little" tasks which, however, were performed out of great love for His Heavenly Father.

St. Paul praises the value of charity that makes all our works meaningful before God. But if charity is lacking, no action will be pleasing to God.

If I have all the eloquence of men or of angels, but speak without love, I am simply a gong booming or a cymbal clashing. If I have the gift of prophecy, understanding all the mysteries there are, and knowing everything, and if I have faith in all its fulness, to move mountains, but without

love, then I am nothing at all. If I give away all that I
possess, piece by piece, and if I even let them take my body
to burn it, but am without love, it will do me no good
whatever (1 Co 13:1-3).

Love is more than having a "pure intention" to please
God in all things. Having a desire to be submissive to God's
sovereignty is the first movement of the Holy Spirit, the first
presence of grace moving us toward God. Being open
toward God's presence, we receive the "infilling" of the
Spirit's gift of *love*. It is tied intrinsically to the Spirit's *faith*
that reveals to our consciousness that God truly loves us. It
builds upon the Spirit's gift of *hope* that allows us to
surrender to God's love.

THE SPIRIT IS LOVE

Love, therefore, is the presence of the Spirit filling us
with the unifying force of God's very own uncreative
energies that unite us with God as we seek to perform every
thought, word and deed for God's glory. "Whatever you
eat, whatever you drink, whatever you do at all, do it for the
glory of God" (1 Co 10:31).

In an outdated spirituality we were taught that it really
made no great difference what we did, as long as we had a
pure intention to please God. A childlike abandonment
seeks in all things to please God and to return love through
the symbols of one's thoughts, words and actions. When
love is the driving force directing these toward God, then
love increases. The Holy Spirit increases our participation
in divine life that allows us to grow more intensely in a
likeness to Jesus Christ into a consciously loving child of
God.

But true love also adds another dimension of faith that

sees each thought, word and deed in the context of our existential life and hence falling somehow under God's providential guidance of our life and that life in relationship to the total plan of salvation. Thus each action that I am to perform is very important when I can knowingly bring it within God's will action, either His deliberative, "signified" will or His permissive will or, to use the phrase of St. Francis de Sales, "the will of God's good pleasure."[3]

A Christian seeks to place himself under the dominance of the Holy Spirit's activities so that in each moment, in each event, in every thought, word and deed, the child of God moves progressively into a "purity of heart," into a conformity of his will with that of his Heavenly Father's. Each act takes on ultimate meaning and becomes the point of recognizing his Heavenly Father as loving Father while he indeed becomes actually more and more His loving child. Each event becomes a diaphanous unfolding of God's presence as loving Father and the "place" for us to exercise love in our surrender to God in that "place." Each event is surcharged with God's loving presence.

For such a Christian the *now* moment is all important. There is the past only insofar as the past is being revealed in the *now,* but then it is no longer past. The future may never arrive, at least as we may fearfully wish to anticipate it, so that too is meaningless before the awesome *now* moment.

No moment is, therefore, banal, boring or just blah! The poetry in the heart of a child of God allows him to see much more of God in each event than most others do. God saturates this *now* with His presence that makes everything everywhere a sacred place for God to surprise us with His love that can never be limited to any special place or time.

The whole world is a living Bible. God is continuously speaking to us His loving Word and loving us in that Word. In such a state of active abandonment to God's presence we find our response. As Jesus saw His Father working in all events (Jn 5:17), so He worked. We, too, in a *synergy,* a working together with God's active will, go forth in maximum creativity. We measure success and greatness by our humble cooperation to work with, for and in God's strength for the sole love of God.

FREEDOM OF THE SONS OF GOD

Jesus came to set us free.

If you make my word your home
you will indeed be my disciples,
you will learn the truth
and the truth will make you free.
. . . So if the Son makes you free,
you will be free indeed (Jn 8:31-32, 36).

We are not born free. This is a progressive gift of Jesus' Spirit that takes away our darkness of lonely isolation and fears, anonymity and lack of true identity by leading us into the state of being true children loved by our Father. We are called to liberty by Christ (Ga 5:13). By becoming children of our Father we become freed from everything that holds us in crippling fear, worry or anxiety. Jesus frees us from our sinful past by forgiving our sins and healing our memories. By His grace we can abandon ourselves to serve God in this present moment, that removes all anxieties about the future.

If we seek to please God in all things, we experience a liberty that opens us up to a multitude of transcendent possibilities that were ruled out earlier because we sought only to serve our self-love or to yield to human respect and the desires of others. Like the four animals of human form in Ezekiel's vision, we go where the Spirit urges us without turning to either side (Ez 1:12).

Jesus was, of all men, the most free, because He sought in the Spirit to please in all things His Heavenly Father. He was the most human of all men, free to love all human beings deeply, as the Father wanted them to be loved. He could enjoy good food (and even poor food!); He enjoyed wine at wedding feasts and banquets and probably also got a bang out of dancing! All creatures shouted to Him of His Father's presence. He was freed of all self-love.

Thus we see true freedom to consist in taking our life in hand and determining its direction by choices illumined by God's Spirit. Childlike abandonment is the measure of how free the Spirit has allowed us to be to make choices in terms of God as our center and sovereign love.

PEACE . . . IT IS I

How often Jesus brought peace to His disturbed Disciples, especially after His resurrection, and to all who were heavily burdened in any way. The positive injunction—"Peace"—and the negative command—"Fear not"—are the effects of surrendering to the freedom that Jesus' Spirit brings us. Most of the lack of peace in our lives comes from seeking our own wills, with no reference to God. St. Francis de Sales often used the example of a cross. It is made up of two pieces of wood crossing each other perpendicularly. If we oppose God's will, we have a cross. If we place our will alongside that of God, in conformity to His, there are only harmony and peace.

Peace, coming from surrendering ourselves to please God in all things, is beautifully illustrated by Psalm 23:

Yahweh is my shepherd,
  I lack nothing.
In meadows of green grass he lets me lie.
  To the waters of repose he leads me;
There he revives my soul.

He guides me by paths of virtue
  for the sake of his name.

Though I pass through a gloomy valley,
  I fear no harm;
beside me your rod and your staff
  are there, to hearten me.

. . . Ah, how goodness and kindness pursue me,
  every day of my life;
my home, the house of Yahweh,
  as long as I live!

St. Augustine defined peace as the tranquility of order.[4] Man reaches the rest of the "seventh day" (Heb 3:10) by obedience to God's will, not by disobedience. Man reaches a state of equilibrium when he knowingly is living as a loving, obedient son of His Creator and Father. Dying to sin and pride, he is free to be the person God wants him to be. Abandonment brings a continued state of peace and harmony in the relationship between God and man and man with the world around him.

THAT YOUR JOY MAY BE FULL

All people seek joy. It results from the actualizing of our deepest hopes. When we possess what we ardently hope for, joy results. Jesus prayed that His joy might be in us and our joy might be complete (Jn 15:11). All human beings want joy but most place their joy in limited creatures, persons or things, which when sought for themselves can only leave us stale with a taste of what could have been.

The sign of a child's being admitted into God's Kingdom is the joy that radiates in his life, that no man or event can ever take from him because it is rooted as a gift of the Spirit (Ga 5:22) in his surrender to God's holy will.

St. Paul makes it an imperative. "I want you to be happy, always happy in the Lord; I repeat, what I want is your happiness" (Ph 4:4). This is the result of living our Baptism. As we die to the dark areas of selfishness, fears and anxieties, we rise to a new life in the risen Lord Jesus. Joy is the result. And this joy grows stronger as we let go of our lives and yield them to God's control. ". . . you are already filled with a joy so glorious that it cannot be described, because you believe; and you are sure of the end to which your faith looks forward, that is, the salvation of your souls" (1 P 1:8-9).

These are the signs of the children of God who have accepted God's gift of Himself in Christ Jesus and are cooperating with God's grace to return the gift of themselves to God at all times and in all circumstances. These alone are the signs of God's presence among men, for they shout out what all human beings suspect deep down, below their habitual fears. They are proof of the Good News that God so loves us as to give us His only Son Jesus (Jn 3:16) and proof of the paradox that Jesus came to make a living reality: when you lose your life and surrender it toally to God, you will truly find it. Give away your life into God's hands and you will find God in your life. You will be one with God and no one can ever take Him from you.

5

Christian Abandonment

The aim of this chapter is to bring together the basic teaching on Christian abandonment as it has been taught within the Catholic Church throughout the centuries. Just as love has always been taught as the key virtue without which we cannot be Christians, so abandonment to God's holy will has aleays been connected with love. It cannot, therefore, be something newly discovered for our own times or something for past times. During the first four centuries when martyrdom was so common or during the seventeenth century as a true teaching formulated against Quietism and Jansenism, abandonment was equally taught. There is a constant teaching that runs throughout the works of all spiritual writers. There can be, however, particular accents given by certain writers of a certain period, but basically through all ages there has been a common foundational teaching that we would like to present here.

It has always been accepted in Christian piety that the end of our lives is so to grow in faith, hope and love, gifts given to the humble by the Holy Spirit, that we will always seek to conform our will to that of God's will. Jesus taught us that that was His supreme end—to do not His will, but that of His Heavenly Father. He taught us not only to recite but to live the *Our Father* . . . "Thy Kingdom come, Thy will be done, on earth as it is in Heaven."

DOING THE WILL OF THE FATHER

For a Christian, therefore, there is no greater joy than to seek out and do willingly the will of the Heavenly Father. The secret of a truly happy and successful life is gauged by a Christian in terms of seeking, as Jesus always did, to please the Heavenly Father in all things. It is basic human understanding that if we love another, we will "die" to our own wishes and live to please the other. We will seek to do the will of that person.

Thus for Christians true love is not proved by words, no matter how much we may say, "Lord, Lord," but by deeds, by keeping the commandments of God.

> If you keep my commandments
> you will remain in my love,
> just as I have kept my Father's commandments
> and remain in his love (Jn 15:10).

This is not a humiliating submission before a powerful, austere God, but a filial surrender to a loving Father whose loving activities surround us from all sides at all times. Doing His will is the source of our joy.

St. Teresa of Avila writes about the conformity of our will to that of God as the true index of our spiritual progress:

> All that the beginner in prayer has to do—and you must not forget this, for it is very important—is to labour and be resolute and prepare himself with all possible diligence to bring his will into conformity with the will of God. [1]

Because God is supreme and sovereign cause of all that happens, it is justice that demands obedience to God's will. All inanimate creatures, all plants and animals *must* obey God's will. Only man can freely return the gift of his being. This is where man begins the process of growing in love. But the lowest level of love is to fulfill the basic commands of God. This is to resign ourselves to obey God. This is not yet abandonment. It is only the beginning of a long process. St. Bernard calls this the stage of beginners who labor as slaves under fear of a terrifying master.

ABANDONMENT MEANS LOVE

Abandonment of oneself to let God have complete freedom to do with us what He wishes is a movement of grace that admits of many degrees and manifestations. It is not a static relationship to God nor is it a passive surrendering of all activities and desires on our part. St. Paul writes:

> . . . it is by faith and through Jesus that we have entered this state of grace in which we can boast about looking forward to God's glory. But that is not all we can boast about; we can boast about our sufferings. These sufferings bring patience, as we know, and patience brings perseverance, and perseverance brings hope, and this hope is not deceptive, because the love of God has been poured into our hearts by the Holy Spirit which has been given us (Rm 5:2-5).

It is the unfolding of the infusion of the Holy Spirit's gifts of deep faith in the Father's immense love for us, made manifest in Christ Jesus, and of confident trust or hope to let go of ourselves. Trust leads us to this childlike love that is called abandonment. St. Therese of Lisieux has articulated in simple language for Christians of the 20th century what this abandonment meant to her.

> I have now no longer any desire except that of loving Jesus unto folly. Yes, it is love alone that attracts me. I no longer desire suffering nor death, and yet, I love both. I have desired them for a long time. I have had suffering and I have come close to dying. . . . Now, abandonment is my only guide. I can no longer ask ardently for anything except that God's will may be perfectly accomplisehd in my soul.[2]

Abandonment is to live out our Christian Baptism by passing over through filial trust in God's infinite goodness from self-containment to yield ourselves completely according to God's will. St. Francis de Sales writes that it is a true death to whatever we may wish or desire in order to abandon ourselves totally to the good pleasure of Divine Providence.[6]

This act that flows from a progressive growth in love for God is rooted in the unshakeable conviction that all things lie under God's power and that He wills only out of His nature that is *love.* God cannot will anything out of any motive less than His desire to share His goodness with man. His will is always turned towards ultimate good. If it is true as St. Paul says, "What God wants is for you to be holy" (1 Th 4:3), then all that falls under His guiding Providence ought to benefit us unto our eternal good and happiness.

THE SIGNIFIED WILL OF GOD

Scholastic tehologians have distinguished between God's *regulative* and His *operative* will.[4] As regulative, God's will is the supreme rule of goodness. The guiding will of God regulating all that happens is always good. What is good is what God wills. As operative, God's will is the universal cause of every effect. Every effect needs a cause. Without God's will operating to create a being in existence and sustaining it in its form of existence there would be no creatures.

Theologians give another distinction allowing us to speak about God's deliberative and permissive wills in regard to effects produced. This is the distinction between God's *signified* will and that of His *good-pleasure*. The first touches the areas that man can reasonably ascertain as coming under God's expressed will. These can be His direct commandments, both manifested through revelation found in Holy Scripture or through the Church, or His inspirations that touch more particularly a given individual or community.

St. Francis de 'Sales describes God's signified will:

> Christian doctrine clearly sets forth the truths God wants us to believe, the blessings he means us to hope for, the punishments he intends us to fear, the things he would like us to love, the commandments he means us to keep and the counsels he wishes us to follow. All that goes by the name of God's "declared" will, because he has declared and revealed to us that he means and expects us to believe, hope, love and perform it all. [5]

In the area of inspirations, God's signified will is not so clearly discerned. Hence greater sensitivity to God, His commandments and one's duties of life and self-knowledge are needed to "listen" to God's will. The Holy Spirit leads us into such inspirations by producing His fruit of love, peace, joy, patience etc. (Ga 5:22).

GOD'S GOOD-PLEASURE

The *good-pleasure* of God calls for our conformity by submitting to whatever falls under such an expression of God's will. It is where love moves us, not only to obey God in every manifestation of His will in His commands and inspirations, but to surrender to His expressed or permissive will so that our desiring passes away, or better it becomes one with whatever happens to us. Because such a happening comes under the good-pleasure of God, we wish it totally by surrendering ourselves to embrace it with joyful love.

Some authors like J.P. De Caussade, S.J. and Pierre Teilhard de Chardin, S.J. speak only of active and passive acceptance of God's will. De Caussade writes:

The active practice of fidelity consists in accomplishing the duties imposed on us by the general laws of God and the Church and by the particular state of life which we have embraced. Passive fidelity consists in the loving acceptance of all that God sends us at every moment. [6]

Perhaps we can better bring such traditional distinctions together by looking at the will act involved on the part of God and of ourselves. God's *signified* will is an expression of God's commands or wishes to which we are to respond with an active cooperation. The concept of God's *good-pleasure* or *complacency,* in literature on abandonment, can become quite confusing. From the human viewpoint of cooperation with God's providential willing, which functions not always by an actual, deliberative willing, but often only by His permissive will, man has two areas open to him, both of which fall under God's *good-pleasure.*

As Jesus sought to please His Heavenly Father (Jn 8:29), a will act beyond performing the commands and wishes actively expressed by the Father, so man can *actively* push his filial submission to God the Father by wishing to improvise ways of expressing his love by going beyond the expressed will of God. This embraces the whole area of "creative suffering," where man freely chooses symbols that cost him a price in personal self-sacrifice to incarnate his interior love for God. A simple act of kindness freely chosen to do for one in need, some fasting performed, would not be seen as an expression of God's wish but an active desire on the part of man, all other things being equal, to choose what costs more to personal comfort in order to offer a free gift to God.

The other area is man's *passive* acceptance of what apparent evils God permits or could even wish to happen to him in His unscrutable divine Providence. This is perhaps the largest area of man's surrendering of himself continually in the events of each moment to God's will of *good-pleasure.* In this area we can see how we can change what is a low degree of accepting God's will in unpleasant happenings from a mere passive acceptance to a conformity of our will to God's by an intense activity on our part, an exercise of creative abandonment that actively *wants* what is happening. A. Rodriguez, S.J. in his classical work read by so many religious in their novitiate training, *On the Practice of Christian Perfection,* describes this change from passive resignation to an active, loving desire to bring our will in conformity to that of God:

> Third degree: In this degree, which is the most perfect of all, we are not content with just accepting and suffering cheerfully, for the love of God, all the trials He may send us; but in the ardour of our love we long for these trials and

rejoice at their advent, because we know they come from the hand of God and are ordained by His adorable will. [7]

ELEMENTS OF ABANDONMENT

Most authors see abandonment as the bringing together of all Christian virtues into one elan of love toward the Heavenly Father. It is a synthesis of all virtues and the culmination of the working of the Holy Spirit to effect in us a melange of perfect faith, hope and love. Bossuet sees in abandonment "a bringing together and a composition of the acts of most perfect faith, the most complete and most abandoned hope and the most pure and most faithful love." [8]

Its essence is a renunciation of all self-centeredness in order, out of love for God, to do what is perceived by the mind enlightened by grace to be the will of God. It is a total gift of oneself as man, in life's situations, seeks to live according to the mind of God. Love is the key word in abandonment. But when has one loved sufficiently? Thus also abandonment admits of a continued process of self-surrender as one grows in greater love of God.

St. Bernard insists that the measure in which we love God is to love Him without measure so that "once love has taken hold of the heart it carries all before it and renders captive all other affections." [9]

EXTENSION OF ABANDONMENT

Abandonment in its highest degrees extends to anything and everything of the past, present and future. This covers man in all his possible human experiences from birth to death. How difficult it is for most of us to let go of worries and anxieties stemming from our past. Even to let go of the joys of the past with detachment is most difficult. The future, however, looms before us, exciting and foreboding. Before the future becomes this present moment, it dances before our dreamy eyes with ever-changing forms, lovable and desirable, fearful and not wanted.

We give obedience to God's *signified* will that we have knowledge of, most especially in the present but which also extends itself to the future. But strictly speaking abandonment looks to self-surrender to God's will of good-pleasure that touches the past and present, but more predominantly the future. We surrender to whatever God wills or permits to happen in today's events or in those of the near or far distant future.

It enjoins upon us the attitude that St. Ignatius speaks of in his *Spiritual Exercises* as *indifference.* It is a mental state of holding ourselves open to move freely toward whatever God's will indicates, in spite of any natural inclination or affection to the contrary. It is a refusal to act upon mere natural drawing or desire without placing one's deliberative will under submission to whatever God may wish. The term has negative overtones and can ben-conceived of as a stepping-stone to loving abandonment. Abandonment presupposes indifference as a preparation. Thus abandonment, like indifference, embraces as object, all temporal things that touch the well-being of man's body and mind. This would include prosperity and adversity, riches and poverty, individual and public calamities, helath and sickness, life and death, reputation, honors and humiliations. It embraces also all spiritual goods, the life of grace, practice of virtues, failures and sins, temptations, consolations and aridities, trials and desolation.

St. Francis de Sales summarizes the object of indifference leading to a loving acceptance of God's good-
pleasure in all things of the body, soul and spirit, past,
present and future:

> Disinteredness is to be shown in natural things, such as
> health, sickness, beauty, plainness, weakness, strength; in
> social life, such as honors, rank or wealth; in the ebb and
> flow of the spiritual life, such as dryness, encouragement,
> enthusiasm, boredom; in activity, in suffering—in a word,
> whatever happens.[10]

MAN'S ACTIVITIES

One must not confuse true abandonment with a false
form of Quietism (more of this later in this chapter). St.
Ignatius, who so strongly urges *indifference* as a fruit to be
obtained by making the *Spiritual Exercises,* could also
write:

> Rely on God by doing everything as though the success
> depended entirely on you and not on God. And, moreover,
> while using all of your efforts to succeed in the given matter,
> do not count on those but only as if God alone must do it all
> and you nothing.[11]

We have been created, not as automatons, but as
human beings with intellect and will. True love is possible
only with man's cooperation. St. Augustine who preached
so eloquently the harmonious interaction of grace and
man's cooperation in loving faith and hope, wrote: "He
that created thee without thy knowledge will not save thee
without thy consent."[12]

It is clear from Jesus' teaching in the Gospel that we

must strive to do God's will at all times, never being
anxious and over-solicitous about anything. Still He insists
on our need to cooperate and do all God would wish us to
do to obtain what we believe in according to God's will. He
also insists that we pray to the Heavenly Father. How can
we be indifferent and still be inclined through prayer to
desire one definite outcome?

We all normally desire health, not sickness, to live
rather than to die. Does true abandonment permit our
desiring and praying for such? This is perhaps the most
delicate area needing discernment in prayer. St. Ignatius in
his *Spiritual Exercises* and in his *Constitutions* constantly
uses the phrase, "After having gone to prayer . . ." In
prayer we learn what to pray for. We purify our hearts to
receive the Holy Spirit's inspirations that God is
"signifying" His will for us, inclining us toward this rather
than that. If in prayer, we see that we desire to pray for
health in order to work for God's greater glory, this intention in prayer is effecting what our abandonment seeks
to accomplish—to do more perfectly what will redound to
God's greater glory.

We trust that God will provide for what we are to eat
and put on but that means someone has to prepare the food
and put the clothing on us. God will provide us with health
but it may mean an operation and a stay in the hospital. We
can pray and trust God will provide us with a job but His
will directs us to knock on doors and seek employment.
Parents must love their children but they must also make
efforts to correct them.

God is to be found in a trusting abandonment to His
holy will, but His will demands that we exercise prudence in
doing all we can do to promote God's will. Part of God's
order is that we do all that depends on us. What God wishes

is our childlike abandonment to His loving providence in that we avoid all excessive solicitude and anxiety in seeking things other than the Kingdom of God.

PRAYING FOR SUFFERING

What are the limits of prudence in the opposite direction? Does abandonment allow us to pray for trials and sufferings? We have mentioned "creative suffering," an active seeking from time to time an act that costs us a price in personal self-denial in order to seek to please the Father and to return His great love.

There have been saints who have prayed for sufferings. That such a desire could be a very special inspiration is possible. A holy and intelligent spiritual director and a loving, supportive community are the best help in such discernment. The doctrine of abandonment, however, does not include this as essentially a characteristic of one who practises total abandonment. This may be a special *charism* for individual persons in certain conditions of life. If it is a special inspiration from God, this must be discerned with great prudence and be unto the glory of God.

DEGREES OF ABANDONMENT

In the sense that all Christians are obligated to correspond to the graces of the Holy Spirit of faith, hope and love, we can affirm that all are universally called to practise abandonment. All are obligated to conform their wills to that of God. But this admits of various degrees of perfection. Just as we are all enjoined to be perfect, yet few attain to heroic sanctity as a state of life, so, too, not all attain to a highly developed degre of abandonment totally in all things to God's good-pleasure.

But even any given individual Christian should be progressing to a more perfect degree of abandonment as he advances in the spiritual life. God's action becomes more predominant as the Christian grows in greater faith, hope and love. Our action becomes a non-doing, an active receptivity to God's loving presence. God reveals Himself more powerfully. Our response is to empty ourselves of all control over the love relationship, first on the level of discursive thought that yields to a simplification of faith with a resting before God's freedom so that He who loves us so much now can have His full sway over us.

Basically authors describe three principal degrees of abandonment. 1. The first degree exhibits a promptitude in accepting joyfully all external events that happen to us as well as interior states of consolation or desolation, presence or absence of God, aridity and spiritual trials.

2. The second degree is to enter into such a simplifies state of love that it is characterized by the term "spiritual childhood." It is an imitation of children who enjoy a joyful, trusting abandonment of themselves to their parents who seek in all things the well-being of their children. This is the degree that St. Therese of Lisieux so well exemplified for the modern world not only by describing in her writings but above all by living it in her brief Carmelite life. She writes:

Jesus is pleased to show me the one and only road that leads to the Furnace of Love. This is the abandonment of a little child that goes to sleep without fear in the arms of his Father.[13]

3. The highest degree is the "state of abandonment."
De Caussade describes this state in a letter:

> If you wish to be perfect, strip yourself of all your own
> views, of all pretensions, of all self-seeking, of all thought of
> yourself, of all that you can call *yours,* and abandon
> yourself without reserve and once and for all to the direction
> and good pleasure of God. Self-abandonment, yes, com-
> plete self-abandonment, blind and absolute, is for souls
> who are walking in your path the height and sum of per-
> fection, for perfection consists in pure love and for you the
> exercise of pure love consists in self-abandonment.[14]

THE FRUIT OF ABANDONMENT

The chief importance of abandonment is that God
exercises complete sovereignty in the life of the Christian
who practices this as an habitual state. Obstacles to grace
stemming from one's selfishness and attachment to one's
own will are removed. An attitude of total receptivity to
God's action in one's interior as well as in his exterior life
leads the Christian to the highest level of love which con-
tains in its nature all other virtues.

Lehodey sketches the fruit of such totally disinterested
love.[15] It brings a deep and tender intimacy with God. He
is experienced as love and yet uniquely as loving Father
giving His loving Son, Jesus, who releases the Holy Spirit
who constantly divinizes us into children of God (Rm 8:15;
Ga 4:6).

The Christian experiences a simplicity and liberty that
approach that enjoyed by Jesus who centered His whole
earthly life on doing only the will of His Father. Such a
person is freed from himself, unfettered from inordinate

passions and attachments. External forces like poverty, sickness, humiliations, tribulations of any kind, even those interiorly experienced, have no power to frighten him. The words of St. Paul are his for neither death nor life, no created thing "can ever come between us and the love of God made visible in Christ Jesus our Lord" (Rm 8:39).

Constancy and equanimity are the effects of being rooted in the unchangeable love of God. Whims and selfish feelings have no voice in determining man's attitudes and ways of acting, since only God's will is sought at all times. Grounded in such stability, one enjoys peace and joy that no man or event can ever take from him. The Lord rules him. He shall want nothing (Ps 23).

FALSE ABANDONMENT

Throughout the history of Christianity the teaching and practice of abandonment have always been open to abuses. In the temporal order, literalists who apply Jesus' words (Mt 6:25) in too passive a sense err often by producing a laziness and a lack of foresight. Believing that it gives God greater glory not to do anything but to seek the Kingdom of God, as did the Messalians of Asia Minor in the 5th and 6th centuries, such Christians expect society to provide for their material needs. As we have pointed out above, God's Providence expects us to do what we can to cooperate with His designs.

Often an antinomian attitude that wars against any structure or law in Christianity takes over as was seen among the Brethren of the Free Spirit and the Beghards in the Germanic and Flemish lands of the 14th century.

In the spiritual order we see an exaggerated passivity that throughout the centuries has been called *Quietism.*

This heresy reached its peak in its doctrinal expression and practices in the 17th century in such personages as Francis Malaval, Pier Matteo Petrucci, Miguel Molinos and to some extent in the writings of the semi-Quietists, Madame Guyon, Lacombe, La Mothe, and Fenelon. Contemplation as so much of their writings had it, had brought them into a passive state of mystical union that put them beyond temptation, sin and the need of exercising virtues or receiving the sacraments.

The error of such abuses lay in suppressing all action on the part of the individual Christian. Such excessive abandonment brought the Quietists to become indifferent even to their salvation, which contradicted the expressed will of God who seeks always our salvation and with our cooperation.

ABANDONMENT—THE END OF OUR LIFE

True abandonment is the sign of true love for God since self-surrender puts us completely at the disposition of God. Through a living faith in God's infinite love for us we are able to trust in that divine love to work constantly to bring us into the fullness of life and happiness. We trust in God in all our needs. This leads us through a constant detachment from everything but from God's holy will, expressed in the events of each moment to a state of continuous, loving surrender to God. Indifferent to all persons and things in order to live totally for love of God, the Christian experiences in a marvelous way that God does not abandon him but reveals Himself as a loving Father in ways that cannot be expressed in human words. What Christian abandonment means in its best expression is given in a famous prayer of abandonment by Charles de Foucauld:

Father, I abandon myself into your hands. Do with me what you will. And for whatever you may do, I thank you. I am ready for all. I accept all. Let only your will be done in me and in all your creatures. I wish no more than this, O Lord. Into your hands I commend my life. I offer it to you with all the love of my heart. For I love you, God, and so need to give myself, to surrender myself into your hands without reserve, and with boundless confidence, for you are my Father.

6

Discovering God In The Event

To do the will of God is to enter into the healing process of becoming what the Father has always seen us to be in His Son, Jesus:—His loving children. To live outside a conscious oneness with the Father's will is to live in a world of illusions. It is one and the same thing, not to live according to the loving mind of God and not to recognize and live according to our true dignity as His children.

But where do we find the Heavenly Father, through His Holy Spirit, "unconcealing" His mind in order to lead us into true freedom as His sons and daughters? We have earlier pointed out how Jesus abandoned Himself to His Father in the context of His daily life. He found His Father unveiling Himself as Love, pouring Himself completely into the Son's being and calling Him into His Sonship in each moment. Jesus found His Father working always and He Himself wanted to work in union with Him (Jn 5:17). He does nothing at any time of Himself but only in the Father's power and love in order to please Him (Jn 5:19).

A PROCESS THEOLOGY OF EVENT

Many so-called "Process thinkers," such as Alfred

Whitehead, Henri Bergson, Charles Hartshorne, Daniel Day Williams, Norman Pittenger, Gabriel Marcel and Schubert Ogden, view the world in an evolving process. Fixed, static natures of God, man and all other creatures yield to an open-ended society of beings that are living, changing, developing, acting on and being acted upon by an endless number of relationships.

In such a vision of reality, the world and all creatures belong to a society of inter-related "occasions." There can be no isolation or withdrawal and still be a growth unto greater *being.* Into each occasion, past events as well as present pressures enter and open us to the excitement of the next future moment.

Norman Pittenger writes:

> We live in and we are confronted by a richly inter-connected, inter-related, inter-penetrative series of events, just as we ourselves are such a series of events.[1]

GOD'S UNCREATED ENERGIES

Such a process theology is not new among Christian thinkers. Among the great mystic-theologians of Eastern Christianity, such as St. Basil, St. Gregory of Nyssa, St. Maximus the Confessor, St. Symeon the New Theologian, and St. Gregory Palamas, we find God described in His *graceful* relationships with us and His whole created order as *uncreated energies.* They did not oppose *nature* to *supernature* but rather the natural as opposed to the un-natural.

Man was made "according to the Image and Likeness" of God, Jesus Christ (Gn 1:26, Col 1:15) in a process of continued growth. As he yields to the divinizing process of

Jesus Christ and the Holy Spirit bringing him to a greater consciousness of his sonship to the Heavenly Father, he enters into his true nature to become "a partaker of the divine nature" (2 P 1:4).

Such Fathers taught that God, like the sun, sends off His uncreated energies, as rays of light and warmth, to touch us and inter-act with us and through us with the rest of creation. Although Scripture tells us that no man has ever seen God and lived (Jn 1:18; 1 Jn 4:12), that His essence is totally unknowable and inaccessible to man, yet He gives Himself through His energies. These are not "accidents," but are truly God in His loving relationships to mankind. God is always, therefore, acting *naturally,* according to His nature as loving Father. He never begins to work supernaturally.

Thus God in His energies permeates every material atom of this universe. For Him and the Christian enlightened by faith, everything is God gifting of Himself to man. The whole universe is bathed in the grace of His divine energies. Whether we are eating, loving one another, sleeping or working, God is powerfully present and working as He gives Himself in His energies. Everything is *sacred* for one who has eyes to see God working his His energies. For one of no faith, everything is *profane* and lacking in ultimate meaning. Such a person believes he is alone, separated from God and other persons.

For the believer, however, he is an *I,* aware of God's in-breaking love and aware of responding to His loving energies in each given moment.

THE EVENT

Such a Christian process vision finds God working in all things by His grace, His uncreated energies, touching man and drawing him always into a more intimate union with Himself. It is a vision that takes man from darkness and places him fully in the light of God's loving presence as the Ground of all being. It is a true "unconcealment," an uncovering of what is always there but our lack of faith keeps us from communicating with the ever-present and ever-loving God.

Faith, the work of the energizing Holy Spirit, rips off the false masks from ourselves and others. In a gentle security of knowing we are loved by the all-perfect God, we let go of our need to interpret events or happenings according to our darkened ideas that we entertain, especially of our false *ego*. Not having a true love of ourselves because our faith is not strong enough to convince us of God's love for us unto death in His Son Jesus, we fashion opinions of ourselves and the world around us that are simply a lie and do not present the "really real" as God sees it.

The *event* is, therefore, whatever is happening to us. The word is derived from the Latin word, *evenire*, to come out of. It dynamically presents us with a given moment out of which something is coming, being brought to birth. By faith we can say that God is coming out of this or that moment. What is happening *now* is that God is calling us to find Him in that happening moment. God has not been sleeping and He now wakes up and "comes out" of the event as a butterfly emerges from the darkness of the cocoon. God has been there all the time, loving and giving Himself in the moments that preceded and prepared this moment.

It is man who has been sleeping and totally unaware of the richness of God's love in those preceding moments, going back to his birth. Now faith stirs him to awaken to God's inner presence. From man's side, he goes *into* the event, he discovers by a finding inside the event what was already stored there. As God comes out of (*evenire*), man goes into (*invenire*) and there in the given moment takes place the loving union of two wills becoming one.

In each event of each moment God is calling man into reality out of his shadowy existence. Our greatest work in life is the asceticism of listening to God's call with utter openness and sincerity. It is a receptive readiness to swing freely wherever God leads. "Speak, Lord, thy servant hears" (1 S 3:10). Our most difficult ascetical struggle comes in what the Fathers of the Desert call *nepsis,* the constant, interior vigilance we exercise over every thought, feeling, imagination that could possibly throw us out of the faith dimension of being in Christ, back into the darkness of insecurity and fear.

In each event we discover by a new, positive awareness that we really are children of God (1 Jn 3:1). We learn in the event to let go of negativity and we find the godly and the truthful in each moment. We learn to yield gently to God's loving presence in ourselves so that we think and act as whole, healed persons, for that is what God sees us to be in His love for us. Aggressiveness against others disappears as we gently let the presence of God come forth. God in us meets the God in others and we discover the freeing joy that the Spirit has made us one in Christ.

THE PRESENT MOMENT

For such a *faith-full* Christian, seeking the face of God in each event, it is this present moment in which he finds a new incarnation. Or perhaps it would be more true to say that God is again taking on "flesh," breaking into our world to pitch His tent among us, to bring His *shekinah* of infinite glory into our darkened world. Or simply we can say that Jesus is being "unconcealed" for us for, since His first incarnation, He has never really left us.

In this present moment God and man meet in the Incarnate Word. Jesus Christ as Teilhard de Chardin says, "by the name of the Resurrection" is caught forever inside matter. He touches it and reconciles it back to the Father through you and me finding in this present moment what the Father has eternally seen in His loving Word. The historical time of this *now* moment (the *chronos*) is transvected by the eternal now of God's healing (*salvific*) love (the *hairos*). God's grace in His uncreated energies of God touch man's free will and the Body-Being of His only begotten Son, Jesus, is extended again into space and time.

FEAR LEADS TO THE UNREAL

Jesus knew that all of us tend toward fears, worries and anxieties. In our isolation and ignorance, not knowing of our inner beauty as loved already by God so infinitely in Christ Jesus, we take things, events into our own hands. We interpret them according to our self-centered fears.

Blaise Pascal in a well-known text comments on how we live under fear of the past or the future and thus lose the only contact we have with reality:

> We never hold ourselves to the present time. We anticipate the future as coming too slowly in order to hasten its advent. Or we recall the past in order to stop its passage too rapidly. Too imprudently we err in times which are not ours and we do not think of what only is in our power, what truly does belong to us.
>
> So in vain do we hanker for those things which are no more and thus we let fly away, without batting an eyelash, the

only thing that exists. This is the present which ordinarily wounds us. We hide it from view because it afflicts us. And if it is pleasing to us, we regret seeing it pass.[2]

Thus bound and enslaved to the past and the future in fear, we ignore the present that alone can bring God's healing to the past hurts, loneliness and sinfulness. By opening ourselves in complete abandonment to His loving, creative presence in this *now* moment, we move into the *real* future that no human eye has ever seen nor ear heard nor could it ever have entered into our minds what God has prepared already for those who love Him (1 Co 2:9).

How exciting to realize these things prepared for us are not the static, eternal ideas predetermined by a God who is totally detached from our material world. Rather, our faith in the presence of God in this event calls us into a great adventure. We are called into God's creative, loving energies to co-create with Him out of the raw-stuff of each moment the only *real* world there is, namely, the world of living and loving in His holy will.

THE SACRAMENT OF THE PRESENT MOMENT

If God is "inside" the stuff of each moment, He must be effecting what these *signs* are symbols of—His great self-giving love toward us. J.P. De Caussade, in his classical work on *Self-Abandonment to Divine Providence,* gives us the very suggestive phrase: "the sacrament of the present moment." Sacraments are visible signs made up of material things and gestures along with words that lead the Christians, not only into what the signs signify, but also into an effective encounter with Jesus Christ who brings about what the signs signify.

Through our faith that God is creatively present in each moment, we can therefore believe that He is in an analogous way effecting a sacramental self-giving to the Christian, thus bringing him into a greater union with Himself.

In the sacrament of the Holy Eucharist the priest breathes over bread and wine the words: "This is My Body ... This is My Blood." Through the calling down of the Holy Spirit (in the Byzantine Liturgy this is called the *epiklesis*), the faithful enter into an *unconcealment,* to find that these gifts are no longer mere bread and wine but a *transfiguration* has taken place. This is now the Body and Blood of Jesus Christ. The signs of bread and wine, not only signify that Jesus is our food and drink, but through the action of the Holy Spirit the Father effects again His eternal Gift of Jesus to nourish us into His strong, loving children.

Also in the context of our Christian lives the Holy Spirit gives us faith to see the Body of Christ being formed or better, being *revealed* in the event of each moment. We can thus reverence and adore His sacred presence. As we surrender to His loving activity, God's Spirit reveals to us what Jesus has effected in the primal eucharistic gift of Himself to us on the Cross. In the faith, hope and love with which we encounter God in each moment, we can joyfully relinquish control over our lives, plans, desires for this moment. In total abandonment, we yield to God's dynamic, loving activity in this *now* event.

ILLUMINED BY FAITH

It is not enough for us to open ourselves to God's gift to us of the present moment. By faith we "see" God, get in touch with His loving activities and then work with Him to

effect a transformation to something better. Faith illumines
us in a freeing way to see God inside of the moment. But
there is a freeing by faith also from ourselves and the
limitations that we place upon ourselves and others. The
negativity that believes we and others can do only so much
is transcended by faith so that we can truly shout out to
ourselves and to the whole world: "I can do all things in
Him who strengthens me."

Faith does not lead us into presumption but into a true
assessment of each situation and what we can do with God's
help to change matters according to God's will. True
gentleness and meekness are rooted in humility, seeing
reality through faith according to God's eyes. We can turn
the other cheek to our enemies but God would want us to
work diligently at the same time to transform them by our
love and prayerful intercession into our brothers. Faith
works along with God's gift of human intelligence, but it
allows us to see farther into the tunnel when our own
human knowledge runs out of light.

Faith to believe in God's infinite love is rooted in the
Word of God. We must learn through the illumination of
the Holy Spirit to have an uncompromising openness to
God's call in the history of salvation. It is openness to Holy
Scripture that we are able to enter into a faith act that
convinces us that Jesus Christ is still speaking to us. Our
faith in the Good News and His healing power breaking in
upon us through the event of the present moment comes
from a prayerful knowledge of Scripture.

LIVING THE EUCHARIST

Our Christian faith reaches its peak in the greatest
event or happening, in the Holy Eucharist. In Scripture we
grasp by faith some aspect of Christ's teaching or per-

sonality. In the Eucharist we open in faith to the total Jesus Christ. If we open ourselves to Jesus in the events of Scripture and in the existential Word meeting us in each daily happening, how much more ought we to open ourselves to the Eucharistic Event where Jesus gives Himself to us directly and completely?

It is the peak of communion with the Heavenly Father through Jesus, accomplished as the fruit of Holy Communion, namely, in "the fellowship (*koinonia*) of the Holy Spirit," as the Byzantine Liturgy expresses it. Here is the climax of all other events since the Trinity is directly encountered in our adoration and self-surrender. Here time meets eternity, our fragmented life touches the eternal life of God.

"This is eternal life, that you may know the Father and him who the Father has sent, Jesus Christ" (Jn 17:3). The Heavenly Father so loves us that He gives us His only begotten Son Jesus so that, believing in Him, we might have eternal life (Jn 3:16). All this happens in the Eucharist in order that our joy may be full (Jn 15:11). When we eat of the Bread of Life, we are called into the most intense act of faith to surrender ourselves wholly to Jesus' person, His example and teaching. This, therefore, is the *Event* that builds up the faith necessary to meet the same Jesus in the other lesser, eucharistic events of the day.

We do not receive the Eucharist to speak pretty sentiments to Jesus, although this will also be a part of our loving communion. Through the event of the Eucharist we break out in faith to put on the total mind of the Father, Son and Holy Spirit. In the microcosmic communion with the transfigured Bread and Wine, we are brought into a deeper faith to a cosmic communion, first with the Body of Christ, those members living by faith in Jesus as Lord. We embrace also the whole universe of human beings, inhabiting this planet earth, those already living in the life to come and even in some degree, those yet to come. We believe in the transformation of the entire material cosmos as bread and wine in the Eucharist lead us to a hope that this world, groaning in travail (Rm 8:23), will be also glorified in Christ.

Teilhard de Chardin beautifully prays such a Eucharistic faith in the *Divine Milieu:*

> Grant, O God, that when I draw near to the altar to communicate, I may henceforth discern the infinite perspectives hidden beneath the smallness and the nearness of the Host in which You are concealed. I have already accustomed myself to seeing, beneath the stillness of that piece of bread, a devouring power which, in the words of the greatest Doctors of Your Church, far from being consumed by me, consumes me. Give me the strength to rise above the remaining illusions which tend to make me think of Your touch as circumscribed and momentary. I am beginning to understand: under the sacramental Species it is primarily through the 'accidents' of matter that You touch me, but, as a consequence, it is also through the whole universe in proportion as this ebbs and flows over me under Your primary influence. In a true sense the arms and the heart which You open to me are nothing less than all the united powers of the world which, penetrated and permeated to their depths by Your will, Your tastes and Your temperament, converge upon my being to form it, nourish it and bear it along towards the center of Your fire. In the Host it is my life that Your are offering me, O Jesus.[3]

HOPEFUL EVENTS

As we embrace each event, we open to the loving presence of God. We hope in that loving presence as being one with the unchanging revelation in Christ Jesus of God's undying, infinite love for each of us. Thus each event is charged with God's presence, but as *beyond* and *unreachable* by our own power or merits. We are challenged to take a risk that God will really be *there* when we hopefully seek to encounter Him in this now moment.

Hope allows us to go beyond our own controlled reality as we open in a risk to seek the hidden God. R. Troisfontaine writes:

> In the light of God calling me to personal communion, my whole life is as a test to me, in each of its circumstances; it always includes a temptation and a stake . . . Salvation is to find in every reality its relation to the beyond. The test is that which has a beyond. [4]

In each moment we are called to risk and to live in hope by staking everything on God's loving fidelity to us. We cannot fathom how God will be present in each given event, still we *hope* in His loving presence. We allow Him to possess us totally in each moment. And we can do so because the Holy Spirit *inspires* us, He *breathes* into us a hope in God's goodness and perfect holiness. Our hope is in Him, even as we look at our own poverty and inability to cope with the situation.

Hope in each event lives, therefore, in the dizzying altitudes of the *unfathomableness* of God. We are at peace with our complete surrender to Him. We no longer nervously want to dominate and control ourselves or even God. A gentle openness to other persons and to each event becomes an habitual attitude on our part. As we hope in the unfathomableness of God in this moment, we find ourselves hoping also in the unique unfathomableness of our neigh-

bors. We can now allow their deeper levels of being, that
are beyond the fathoming of our aggressive selves, our
"carnal" minds, to be in touch with our deeper level of
being. We can truly let the other person *be* that unique
individual that God loves, as we hope in God's abiding
presence working in that person's life.

Gabriel Marcel's famous saying becomes a lived experience: "I hope in you for us." Hope in another person is
an assurance given that he or she will never die but we
together will live in God. I hope in a human being because
ultimately I hope in God's love.

The "you" in whom I hope is each of those beings that I
love. It is especially the "You" absolute, the transcendent
. . . Absolute hope is the response of the creature to the
infinite Being to whom it is aware that it owes all it is . . .
He brought me out of nothing.[5]

PRAYING ALWAYS

Ultimately abandonment to God in the event of each
moment brings us into a state of infused prayer that allows
us to "pray incessantly," as St. Paul says (1 Th 5:18). We
live in a constant remembrance of God in His loving self-
giving to us in each moment. Because the Holy Spirit is
pouring into our hearts deeper faith, hope and love, we can
thank God for all things because we will be able to see His
loving goodness in each creature that comes into our life.
Thanking Him for all things at all times, we will be always
united in prayerful adoration and praise.

Praise will be on our lips and in our hearts.

Praise Yahweh, my soul!
I mean to praise Yahweh all my life,
I mean to sing to my God as long as I live (Ps 146:1-2).

We believe that God is "righteous in all that he does. Yahweh acts only out of love" (Ps 145:17).

The sign of a constant praying attitude in each event is the lack of worries and the presence of a *rejoicing* heart. St. Paul describes the relationship between realizing God's nearness, a rejoicing heart and no worries when he writes:

> I want you to be happy, always happy in the Lord; I repeat, what I want is your happiness. Let your tolerance be evident to everyone: the Lord is very near. There is no need to worry; but if there is anything you need, pray for it, asking God for it with prayer and thanksgiving, and that peace of God, which is so much greater than we can understand, will guard your hearts and your thoughts in Christ Jesus (Ph 4:4-7).

Anchored in faith and hope in God, we thus give up fear and worry. We rejoice constantly because God is near us. If He is with us, who can ever be against us (Rm 8:31)? Excessive worry and sadness negate the gifts of the Spirit of faith, hope and love. Christians put aside all negativity and think thoughts of peace, joy and victory in the conquering power of Jesus.

> You have already overcome these false prophets, because you are from God and you have in you one who is greater than anyone in this world (1 Jn 4:4).

In all things, in all events, we should thus be giving thanks to God our Father (Ep 5:20). Prayer is not so much now an act that we perform but it is an habitual awareness that the Holy Spirit is praying in us to the Father and Jesus, His son, by the praise and thanks we give to God in all events (Rm 8:26-28). Thus each moment is impregnated by God's caressing love. All things become an encountering point to reveal God's loving presence. No longer can such a Christian be sad or lonely, for God is truly in all things, communicating His love for him.

Not only will we find God in each moment, but we will in each moment respond to His loving presence. The Eucharist is God's gift of Himself totally to us in His Son Jesus through His Spirit. Our daily lives with each moment are the "place" where we return our eucharistic gift of ourselves to God. This place, this *now* event, is holy for God's holy presence as love to us is unveiled there. It is holy because we respond by the power of the Holy Spirit to become God's holy children.

> Trust in Yahweh and do what is good;
> make your home in the land and live in peace;
> make Yahweh your only joy
> and he will give you what your heart desires.
> Commit your fate to Yahweh,
> trust in him and he will act:
> making your virtue clear as the light,
> your integrity as bright as noon (Ps 37:3-6).

7

Abandonment In Human Love

Jesus came to free us from our blindness. We look through the windows of our eyes at the *phenomenal* world around us. We hear movements, noises, attempts at communication by a stuttering, scared world. We touch a world, but not with the reverence of touching God. Our touch is the grasp of Midas, to transform the world into possessions for power and luxury. We taste and smell a world of beauty and we want more and more to give us an elixir of lasting pleasure. Yet the pleasures grow stale and we turn away bored.

We are in touch with a world that we by and large create according to our needs. Where does the true world lie, the true experience? Who am I? Who are you? Jesus came to bring us life, that we might have it more abundantly (Jn 10:10). He was the light shining in our darkness (Jn 1:4-5). The sad part of our lives is that we do not know that we are in darkness, that the world we think we are seeing and in touch with is not His world.

Once Jesus entered the village of Bethsaida and the people brought to Him a blind man. We read:

He took the blind man by the hand and led him outside the
village. Then putting spittle on his eyes and laying his hands
on him, he asked, 'Can you see anything?' The man who
was beginning to see, replied, 'I can see people; they look
like trees to me, but they are walking about.' Then he laid
his hands on the man's eyes again and he saw clearly; he
was cured, and he could see everything plainly and
distinctly. And Jesus sent him home, saying, 'Do not even
go into the village' (Mk 8:23-26).

Like the blind man, we look at others and see "trees,"
mere objects. We need new eyes to see them. We need a
new *gentle* spirit that will take away our aggressiveness, our
attack against people.

AGGRESSION

Today much more is being written about man's
aggressiveness than about his gentleness. We carefully have
catalogued all the different species of abnormal people, but
rarely do we describe the *normal* person. Movies and plays
revolve around despair and loneliness; few deal with hope
and loving communities.

One reason for so much violent aggression in our
modern world is our sense of insecurity. Rapid movements
bring quick changes. Physically, psychologically and
spiritually we are not always "balanced" enough to cope
with changes. Thus we instinctively use aggression to build
up a security or at least we employ some form of withdrawal.

Not all forms of aggression are evil. We need
aggressively to defend ourselves from any form of attack
that unjustly threatens to destroy us in any physical,
psychological or spiritual way. We flee from a murderer; we

attack in order to control raging forces of nature such as floods and epidemics. A youth aggressively withdraws from parental control in order, hopefully, to discover his important autonomy as a self-directing person. Thus such aggressiveness can be a most necessary defense mechanism for our true development.

But we speak here of an aggressiveness that is destructive to our true growth as human beings. It is rooted in our sinful, false ego as a result of what St. Paul called "sin which lives inside my body" (Rm 7:23). He saw the constant inner conflict between his reason, enlightened by the Holy Spirit, and sin that lived within him. He confessed that when he acted against his will, against that which he knew was right, it was not his *true* self. He is a prisoner of that law of sin living within him. "Who will rescue me from the body doomed to death? Thanks be to God through Jesus Christ our Lord!" (Rm 7:24).

Our false *ego* leads us to believe in the lie that we are unlovable. People are a threat to our false identity so we resort to an aggressive attack to maintain ourselves in a false security. God has made us out of love. We are created according to His very own Image, Jesus Christ, His beloved Son. Jesus has poured His Spirit of love into our hearts (Rm 5:5), but our *ego* does not want us to believe such good news. We use our bodies aggressively to attack individuals or a group or to withdraw. We use our bodies to speak words of offensive power, even to persons we seemingly love. Out of fearful insecurity we refuse a look of love, a touch of tenderness.

Married men and women, having opened themselves sensitively to each other, know how aggressively to "use" the other for their own needs. All of us learn little ways of "surviving" in our false ego's belief that true identity is secured by attack or selfish withdrawal.

YOU ARE A KING

But Jesus comes to release the Father's Holy Spirit to know we have a loving Father and we are His loving children (Rm 8:15; Ga 4:6). We are called by the Father's compassionate mercy and everlasting love "to share the divine nature" (2 P 1:4).

> But you are a chosen race, a royal priesthood, a consecrated nation, a people set apart to sing the praises of God who called you out of the darkness into his wonderful light. Once you were not a people at all and now you are the People of God; once you were outside the mercy and now you have been given mercy (1 P 2:10).

I write these lines on the feast of St. Patrick. Someone sent me a card entitled: "What is it to be Irish?" The answers given can apply to every Christian:

> It isn't only the realization that he is
>   descended from kings.
> It is the realization that he is a king himself. . . .
> It is to walk in complete mystic understanding
> with God for twenty-four wonderful hours.

You have an inner beauty and dignity because you have been reborn, not only of water but also of the Holy Spirit (Jn 3:5). You are beautiful and lovable "because the Father himself loves you" (Jn 16:27). He and His beloved Son have come and made their home in you (Jn 14:23). God so loved you and the whole world, that He gave you His only begotten Son (Jn 3:16). You have, therefore, no need to fear.

In love there can be no fear,
but fear is driven out by perfect love:
because to fear is to expect punishment,
and anyone who is afraid is still imperfect in love.
We are to love, then,
because he loved us first.
Anyone who says, 'I love God,'
and hates his brother,
is a liar,
since a man who does not love the brother that he can see
cannot love God, whom he has never seen.
So this is the commandment that he has given us,
that anyone who loves God must also love his brother (1 Jn
4:18-21).

LOVE YOUR NEIGHBOR

Too often we have been taught a spirituality that teaches faith, hopeful trust and love towards God, but toward human beings, the word is "caution-danger." How many religious have been brainwashed to fear the greatest enemy to their "spousal" oblation of self to God as that of a P.F., a *particular friend?* This teaching came out of a long standing doctrine developed by St. Pachomius and St. Basil, the fathers of early monasticism. The *Long Rules* of St. Basil are a pattern of perfectly logical order. Quoting the words of Jesus (Lk 14:26) about the necessity of hating father, mother, wife and children etc., he insists on an order and interdependence between the commandments to love God and neighbor. This is only one love with a twofold aspect beginning with fear of God and the absolute sovereignty of God over any other human affection.[1]

What most commentators miss in opposing God over human love is that St. Basil equally insists that, *if* and to that degree any human being is an impediment to our total surrender in love to God, then separation is necessary. But he also insists on cultivating friendships that can help us grow in greater love of God.

Throughout the centuries, religious alone were taught this doctrine with particular stress placed on the supremacy of God over all lesser loves. The laity seemed not bound to the "superior" way even though the Gospel injunction of Jesus is of clear obligation on all who call themselves His followers. A distortion of the patristic commentary was that, although we were all obliged to love God supremely, it became accepted that serious Christians, (read: religious), were to love all human beings as *instruments* to prove their love for God and to help them grow in greater Christian love.

The individual with all his or her uniqueness as a *person* never entered into one's giving of love to others. They were *means,* tools to exercise love. The whole incarnational theology that, firstly, God was the transforming power of love within, giving us His love with which to love others, was eclipsed. God loved us. We had to return that love by *our* efforts to love. That any form of true, human, self-forgetting love was possible only by the indwelling uncreated energies of God loving in us was forgotten (1 Jn 4:12, 16).

Secondly, we passed over the great revelation that not only was God's loving presence to be experienced in giving love but His gentle tenderness was to be experienced in receiving His love for us in the love of the other person.

TRUE LOVE—THE SPIRIT'S GIFT

To receive God's love and to surrender ourselves to His indwelling Spirit so as to return our love to God by God's grace means a letting go. This is an on-going process of replacing ourselves as our center of reference with that of God. Only after some years of abandoning ourselves in deep faith that God loves us and in trusting abandonment to let Him be Lord and Master in our lives do we enter upon this threshhold of consciousness, a gift of prayer where we live aware constantly of God's indwelling presence.

At times this love can become very powerful. We think of the joyful ecstasies of a St. Francis of Assisi and a St. Philip Neri crying out, "No more, God!" All other loves and joys melt in comparison to this all-consuming, loving presence of God. At other times it can continue in great fidelity, despite severe aridity and lack of feeling. Such a living, loving relationship with God takes place deep down in the "heart," the deepest level of consciousness informed by grace. It is the actuation of the "imageness" that the Greek Fathers saw as an embryonic life in Christ, given in Baptism and evolved in prayer and fidelity to God's indwelling presence in life's circumstances.

Dr. Carl Rogers, one of America's leading psychiatrists, expresses in modern language the same optimism of the Greek Fathers of the wholesomeness of each human person, deep-down, in his relationship to God.

> One of the most revolutionary concepts to grow out of our clinical experience is the growing recognition that the innermost core of man's nature, the deepest layers of his personality, the base of his "animal nature," is positive in nature, is basically socialized, forward-moving, rational and realistic. [2]

We experience deep down, by the power of the Holy Spirit, that our *true self* is loved constantly by God. This same Spirit brings forth His fruit and gifts so that we are turned outward towards others in love "because the love of Christ overwhelms us" (2 Co 5:14). The Spirit of Jesus in our hearts allows us, not only to know the Father and the Son's presence as loving us, but He impels us in the power of that great love to love other human beings with God's universal love.

Because in prayer we are continually experiencing God's love for us, God's Spirit of love makes us "spiritual" beings. We move beyond the fears and dark anxieties that prevent us from truly letting go and loving others to receive their love. A freeing process takes place as we live a new life of being always in active surrender of our wills to God's will. It is this state of abandonment to God's holy will that prompted St. Augustine to exclaim: "Love and do whatever you wish."

It is not license on our part to love others according to *our* own insecure needs, powerized by *eros* or aggressive attack against persons for our own selfish pleasures. It demands the greatest responsibility in sensitivity to God, to be "recollected" in His loving presence, to be attentive to put to death any creeping forth of selfish love.

UNSELFISH LOVE FOR OTHERS

True love for God brings forth an intense and strong love for others. As we grow in greater awareness of the Indwelling Presence in the deepest center of our being, at the same time we become conscious of this same divine, loving presence in, surrounding and penetrating all other things. The same energizing, loving God, experienced within, is seen in each creature met along the road of life. All things shout out to us that, not only do such gifts from

God show forth, "unveil" a bit of His beauty, but that God is "inside" the gifts. Touching the gifts, we touch the Giver and adore Him. We surrender ourselves to His loving presence in that moment of encountering God in the incarnation of that moment in matter.

Gone are the anxious, aggressive moods to dominate each situation to satisfy our physical and psychic needs. A new global sense of God's presence is discovered in the "sacrament of the present moment." The whole material world reveals God's loving presence in a "diaphany." He shines through the creature. We do not go from the creature to God. The unconcealing is a revelation made only by God's Spirit. He alone shows us God at the heart of matter.

How much more true is God's loving presence as *diaphany* experienced in our unselfish love relationships towards other human beings! Swept up into a oneness with the Trinity dwelling within us, we experience a new founded sense of our own uniqueness as loved by the Father, Son and Holy Spirit. Our true *I* is loved by God as a *Thou*. Only such a loved person is free enough to put aside aggression and attack and be gentle, self-giving and receiving in relations to others.

He knows who he is in God's love. No circumstances can hit him and destroy that identity. God is his Rock! Insults, threats, conflicts from all quarters gather around him yet, like a bastion built on solid rock, he withstands all attacks. He is freed from his false *ego,* screaming lies and casting suspicious doubts about his own identity and that of others. Over all, he remains humble and loving, gently looking into the eyes of each person he encounters to see there the face of God, shining through as Love.

ONE COMMANDMENT

The more we look with non-aggressiveness but with Christ-like gentleness, the more the other person will let go of his walls that he has built up. He will trust us to come in and sup with him. He will lead us beyond the threshhold of his own superficial "outside" shell into the holy of holies. Perhaps he himself has not been aware of God's perfections within himself. He submits to the most exciting experience in human life that admits of an infinite growth. He trusts in us and we hope in him. The God in us embraces the God in him and we all become one in Christ. He is no longer a stranger. He is our brother. He is a part of God's Body! Therefore he is a part of you and me! We discover ourselves in such a love moment.

No longer do we have two commandments: to love God and then to love our neighbor. If we truly are loving God and experiencing His love for us, we will be loving God in all persons and experiencing His love as we accept their love for us.

Such human loves admit of many levels of abandonment. This is to say that to the degree that we experience God's presence in such love relationships, to that degree will we abandon ourselves all the more to His loving activity. In this life, unlike the life to come, we are tied to many basic needs. A child instinctively loves its parents, not because it intuitively in prayer experiences God's loveliness in their self-sacrificing love, but because it needs someone to feed, clothe and love it into greater being.

We can say that we love our children if we are parents or the children we serve in our apostolates, but there, too, are various levels of love. We might selfishly need such children. As adults, we might *use* others whom we say we love. We satisfy our emotional needs by feeding on them, but we do not grow in true, loving self-giving. Certainly, absorbed in ourselves, we do not allow them to grow by our availability to serve them. We easily enough recognize the purity and maturity in our love for another by whether we experience patience or impatience, an openness and readiness to let the other be free to love others or a bilious jealousy that others are threatening our hold on the one we love.

AGAPE

Only God's Spirit can infuse into our hearts true Christian love that is unselfish, humble, serving love toward others. The more our love is of the Spirit, the more it seeks to serve and not to receive for one's selfish needs. It also begins to move out beyond the immediate community to partake of a universal love that opens out to all men and women.

It puts on a gentleness of a loving mother that seeks only to serve and bring out the God-potential in each person encountered.

SPIRITUAL FRIENDSHIPS

Too often such friendships are narrowly limited to celibate religious and often the distinction is made in contrast to love between husband and wife. When the presence or absence of sexual intercourse becomes the distinguishing mark of friendships, we are caught in a faulty view of friendship.

All true friendships, especially among Christians, are fundamentally spiritual, being rooted in the Holy Spirit's love. *Spiritual* indicates the Spirit as the binding force and origin of love between two persons. It must never give the impression that it is negatively so un-incarnate that it is merely a meeting of two detached minds sharing a mutual intellectual interest.

When two people are rooted in God and seek Him above all else, there is a basis for richness. They both seek to surrender themselves to God for they know that only God's Spirit can teach them how to love. To the degree that they have abandoned themselves to God, to that degree they will discover from God how to avoid selfishness and yet how to progress in true love. They learn in their mutual love to find God. Each encounter is like a new discovery of God, loving and revealing Himself through their love. They can say to each other the beautiful words of St. John:

Let us love one another
since love comes from God
and everyone who loves is begotten by God and knows God
(1 Jn 4:7).

Such love may reach a unique level between two persons, but it, rooted in God, can never become limiting and possessively exclusive. Each person is freed by the other to be a similar incarnation of God for many others. Each has in such a friendship experienced the joy of surrendering to God in the other and finds it easy to be open to others.

MAN AND WOMAN

Such friendships, rooted in God, can be powerful and yet beautifully delicate experiences when involving a man and a woman of deep maturity in the Lord. Such can and should be the ideal between husband and wife. When such married persons do grow in the Spirit, their love becomes so deep and freeing and beautiful that they wish to share that beauty with all, a phenomenon that so rarely happens that it seems to prove, alas, that the majority of married people do not grow together deeply in their prayer life and in their surrender to God's Spirit.

Carl Jung has pointed out that every man has locked within his unconscious the *anima* or feminine other self. Each woman possesses the *animus* or masculine other self. This undoubtedly is God working very powerfully in the human psyche to prepare man and woman for mutual growth in seeking their complementarity in the other. "It is not good that the man should be alone; I will make him a helpmate for him" (Gn 2:18).

God has implanted into us the basic need both to be loved and to love, to give love and to receive it. But we do not know how to love as we ought. God is patient with our bungling attempts. He only asks that we be sincere and unselfish, that our love be always patient and kind, never jealous, never conceited, rude or selfish, that it be ready always to excuse, trust, hope and endure whatever comes (1 Co 13:4-7).

As we learn in union with God to take the risk to open to such a person we experience fears and doubts. Danger signs rise up along the way. Which way, Lord? How? What to do and how to say it? Above all, we find a true confrontation with our unredeemed, hidden areas that come out as we see ourselves being mirrored in the openness of the other. Demands of sensitivity and fidelity not known before are made in proportion as we receive the gift of the other. Self can no longer be the center, but we must seek humbly to serve only the unique godliness in the other.

We could hesitate in our human love. The demands might be too great, the sacrifices to self-centeredness too many. The desert of so many unknown and mysterious factors challenges us. Should we dash back to the safe but enslaving days of isolation back in Egypt?

SOME DANGERS

Plato wrote that, to the degree that something can serve to enrich our lives, to that same degree the very same thing can be abused and serve to destroy us. We think of the rich potential for good of atomic energy or its destructive force in the atom bomb. For those who have learned to let go of their hold on their lives and open up to God in another human being, great riches begin to be experienced. How God comes alive in each sharing!

And yet what agony to let go and not hold on to the other! To have reached a oneness in God is to taste a bit of Heaven. To separate from the other is to wrench oneself into two pieces. Abandonment to seek only God becomes an intense moment of decision, constantly repeated, bringing always a new experience of dying to self and rising to a new life in Christ.

One danger in being allowed to share another human being's inner self is that we can be tempted in our selfishness to want the loved one to measure up to our expectations. In love we are gifted to love the other somewhat as God does, in a beautiful hope of what is yet unseen but could be. The one loved has not yet experienced himself or herself as that good, noble or beautiful, yet in the eyes of the lover he or she is already that lovable. One in selfishness can lose this sense of wonder and mystery, poetry and going beyond and settle for impatiently demanding that the other person be more as we would wish or have a need that that person be. We fail to give ourselves to God in His gift as that gift is presented in all of its beauty, potential and actual imperfections.

Martin Buber in his work, *I and Thou,* gives us an Hasidic parable:

> (He) sat among peasants in a village inn and listened to their conversation. Then he heard how one asked the other, "Do you love me?" And the latter answered, "Now, of course, I love you very much." But the first regarded him sadly and reproached him for such words: "How can you say you love me? Do you know, then, my faults?" And then the other fell silent, and silent they sat facing each other, for there was nothing more to say. He who truly loves knows, from the depths of his identity with the other, from the root ground of the other's being he knows where his friend is wanting. This alone is love.[3]

Patience is the love of God operating in us to give us hope that out of such imperfections something very beautiful can result. It means foregoing our aggressive spirit to pierce beyond the threatening surface to the "place" where God transforms the imperfections of the one loved by the patient love of God in the lover. The lover gives hope to the beloved that the latter is already beautiful and can still be more beautiful. Such a lover wishes to serve that dream and give it creative substance. God's love triumphs most in such patient struggles.

THE BODY—GOD'S TEMPLE

Our bodies are not in themselves holy, the temple of the Holy Spirit. Without the Spirit enlightening our minds to loving relationships, our false *ego* looks upon other persons and sees mere bodies. How often men, walking down the busy streets of our cities, look at physically attractive women and see mere bodies, means for an attack to conquer and possess. Rape is evil because it refuses in its complete violence to see in the other a person; it sees only a *thing* to be crushed.

The Holy Spirit wants to use the human body as a means of communicating love. The human body becomes holy and the temple of the Holy Spirit, as St. Paul says (1 Co 3:16; 6:19), when two people in love wish to offer their bodies as channels of communicating God's love. If husband and wife looked upon their bodies as means of the Holy Spirit's communication of love, then physical intercourse would become a sacred act of mystical union with God and with one another. But for many married persons such an act is something to *do,* an orgasm to be *had,* a means to relieve tension in place of a sleeping pill in order to fall asleep.

For others outside of the married state all human communication involves sexuality, hence our bodies, in some way or other. Looks, words, touches, and embraces have meaning depending on two people and what they wish to communicate through such bodily gestures. When we use our bodies to communicate the Spirit's love, great healing of our isolation and loneliness can be experienced. When we use them to attack there is no Spirit-communication, no true love, but only sin.

TRUE LOVE IS TRUSTFUL ABANDONMENT

If the Holy Spirit is leading us in true love in all of our human relationships, He brings us to an inner freedom that results from dying to our aggressive false ego to be open in gentle receptivity to encounter God in the other. This freedom shows itself in a humility that is able to suppress pride and self-containment and express in look and word that we are in need of others to bring us forth into new being. It is a humble acknowledgement of loving service to bring forth the hidden godly beauty in the others encountered.

Such freedom allows us to give ourselves in hopeful trust that others will accept. Our total availability opens us up to be refused and wounded by others. But because the gentleness of God's Spirit has transformed our isolated powerized *ego*, we are able even to transcend such hurts. The cross of Jesus can be deeply experienced in what God has meant to be one of the most beautiful of human experiences.

And yet the peace and joy that we experience in surrendering to the Spirit of love allow us to swing free from rejected love to seek humbly to be led by the Spirit to offer ourselves to others. They, too, may reject us, use us and hurt us, yet we abandon ourselves to God's Spirit. We know from past experiences of love that the end of our lives is to offer, as Jesus did, ourselves to others in love. There can be no other way to human fulfillment and happiness. The pain and risk involved cannot compare to the healing joy of finding in another human being the presence of God, loving us and calling both of us into a greater union with Him and with each other. Our abandonment to God's love is concretely measured by how ready we are to trust the Spirit in another who offers us the privilege of loving him and her and let go of our isolation to become a community in God's love.

8

As Gold Is Purified By Fire

Most of us human beings are fascinated by butterflies, or am I just projecting my own interest? The rare combinations of bright colors with dark shadowings in the wings, the extended antennas lifted up as though listening to a higher power communicating signals, the mobility as it flies about, now settling on this flower, now on that, all such features at least I find intriguing. But the most intriguing moment in my butterfly interest is the passage that I have witnessed a few times in my life of a chrysalis emerging from the cocoon. It was always an incredible experience to watch the butterfly stretch out its tighly packed wings and fly off. Unbelievable that such beauty had come out of that dull, dark-looking chrysalis; even more, that this beautiful butterfly emerged from the ugly caterpillar!

Faith is the mid-wife that assists us to emerge from rather boring, monotonous events, even those of little or great sufferings and to enter into a new transformation of inner beauty and mobility. Such drying moments are true participations in the resurrected life of Jesus Christ. In the moment of suffering with Jesus Christ, we already enter into a share in His glory (Rm 8:17). As we abandon in loving surrender, we experience a new insertion into the life of Christ.

PRAISE THE LORD

The sign of our emerging unto a new level in Jesus before our loving Father is our readiness to praise God in all circumstances. We readily praise and thank God in prosperity when we happily receive from God health, riches or at least all the temporal things we are in need of: honors, friendship, successes in our undertaking. When such blessings come our way we readily hear Joel's words: "Sons of Zion, be glad, rejoice in Yahweh your God" (Jl 2:23).

But the true Christian learns through the Holy Spirit's infusion of faith, hope and love how to praise God in all seasons, under all circumstances. Praise is what flows from the depths of our being as we surrender lovingly to God who is in all things loving us and showering upon us the gift of Himself in whatever happens to us. With Hannah we can pray:

My heart exults in Yahweh,
my horn is exalted in my God,
my mouth derides my foes
for I rejoice in your power of saving.
There is none as holy as Yahweh. . . .
no rock like our God (1 S 2:1-2).

With Job we can rise above our fears and agonizing sufferings to exclaim: "Though he slay me, yet will I trust in him" (Jb 13:15). As Paul and Silas prayed and sang praises to God from prison (Ac 16:25), so we raise our hands to

Heaven and pray: "We give thanks to God and the Father of our Lord Jesus Christ."

Our ability to rejoice and give praise to God in all prosperity and in all sufferings depends on our child-like faith in God's great love for us. Adversities purify our loving praise so that we praise God always solely because He is good and holy. Adversities allow us to humble ourselves before God that He may raise us up to a new union of love with Him.

> Bow down, then, before the power of God now,
> and he will raise you up on the appointed day;
> unload all your worries on to him, since he is
> looking after you (1 P 5:6-7).

FROST AND COLD, PRAISE THE LORD

We have seen that the *event* of each moment unveils God's loving presence and calls us into a return of love. Such events embrace all happenings to which we, unenlightened by God's Spirit, react in various ways. We so often judge the events with what St. Paul calls the "carnal" mind. We limit God's inbreaking love by interpreting the event according to our own center of reference. We find pleasure in certain circumstances and wish more of it. Other events bring us suffering and pain and we want to avoid such moments, throw off such burdens as soon as possible.

But by faith we can move beyond the surface and appearances of the event to touch the loving hand of the Heavenly Father and praise Him in all events. For such Christians, as we should humbly aspire to be, all things serve to glorify God. The weather of this day, regardless of how it upsets our plans, becomes a point of praising God. How difficult it is to join the three young men in the Book of Daniel and praise God in the frost and cold:

> All things the Lord has made, bless the Lord:
> give glory and eternal praise to him. . . .
> Cold and heat . . . frost and cold . . . ice and snow, bless the Lord (Dn 3:57, 67, 69, 70).

Theologians distinguish between physical and moral evils. Physical evils are all those found in the temporal order of nature such as sickness, infirmities, physical poverty, famine, pestilence, earthquakes, wars, floods, droughts, freezing cold, blazing hot weather, etc. The list is endless of the physical sufferings or evils that can come to us. The final and greatest physical evil that will touch all of us eventually and carry us away is death.

And yet in all of these events, whether we can ever discern what is willed or permitted by God, we must lovingly accept the loving presence of God, even when we cannot understand what good could ever come out of such.

MORAL EVILS

Theologians include in moral evils all forms of sinfulness due to man's free resistance to do God's will. When we turn away in disobedience, we create moral evil which separates us from loving union with God. But sins of men have repercussions as well on the physical levels of nature and in the lives of plants, animals and human beings. We need only think of the destructive, physical evils released by a Hitler, a Stalin, an American President ordering an atom bomb to be dropped on Hiroshima or Nagasaki to destroy hundreds of thousands of lives with untold repercussions in nature and the lives of future generations.

Certainly God cannot deliberately will that any person go against His holy will; hence He cannot will, but only permit moral evils to exist. This means that God as first Cause does not withdraw His sustaining presence when we sin. Still He enters into the essential act of sin only by His permissive will to draw from such sins greater good. Such moral evils fall under God's good pleasure whereby God actively works in His merciful designs to draw such sinners even closer to Him. We see this in the lives of many reformed sinners who reached sanctity by God's sustaining love that drew them heroically to Him. Examples of this are Saints Mary Magdalene, Peter, Paul, Augustine and Matt Talbot.

We must also absolutely will with God to do God's *signified* will and ask confidently that we have God's grace to avoid sin and die in a graceful submission to Him. We cannot, like the 17th century Quietist, Miguel Molinos, advocate a state of indifference and abandonment toward sin, which is an absolute evil in its true essence since such an act takes us from our ultimate goal, God.

PHYSICAL ADVERSITIES

But in the physical order any such evils are not intrinsically taking us from God, our ultimate end. What, then, should be our attitude towards such adversities as sickness, poverty, bodily and mental infirmities, wars, droughts and famines? If God is truly a loving Father, how could He will to take from life a mother's three-year-old child? How can we reconcile His loving omnipotence and still allow dictators down through the centuries to put to death so many thousands of innocent people? If God is good and holy, why so many adversities and sufferings in our lives? If He could show us His love by driving away from us such undesirable things, why does He delay?

What priest or minister does not daily meet from distraught parishioners such questions, especially touching on incurable sicknesses and sudden deaths of loved ones? When we bumble an answer about the Providence of God and His permissive will, deep down we know there is no answer except in the direction of deeper faith, abandonment and love.

GOLD IS PURIFIED BY FIRE

Our own intelligence fails to grasp the complexities of science understood quite clearly by the great scientists. How should we expect to unravel the complexities of evil that involve the free will actions of so many human agents? With Job, purified and humbled in his sufferings, we must bow our understanding in loving adoration to that of God:

> I know that you are all -powerful:
> what you conceive you can perform.
> I am the man who obscured your designs
> with my empty-headed words.
> I have been holding forth on matters I
> cannot understand,
> On marvels beyond me and my knowledge.
> . . . I knew you then only by hearsay;
> but now, having seen you with my own eyes,
> I retract all I have said,
> and in dust and ashes I repent (Jb 42:2-6).

God is love and in all His actions, in all His ways, He

must be leading us in love. If we do not understand the *how*, faith and complete trust in His love must bring us into a loving, joyful surrender. Today in some Christian circles there is the belief that God is so good and loving He never wishes to punish us. All sicknesses are from evil powers, all unpleasant events occur from demonic powers. But we forget what Holy Scripture so clearly tells us about God's purifying love. God can never impose a physical or moral evil upon us insofar as it is evil, a negation of *being*.

God can only act out of love. Yet the physical evils of the temporal order God can surely bring about to correct and discipline us so we will return to Him. Scripture so clearly teaches us how God loves us when He prunes us, all in order that we can bear more fruit (Jn 15:1-2). God says without any ambivalence: "I am the one who reproves and disciplines all those he loves" (Rv 3:19; Pr 3:12).

We have already quoted from Heb 12:5-12. "For the Lord trains the ones that he loves and he punishes all those that he acknowledges as his sons. Suffering is part of your training; God is treating you as his sons" (Heb 5:6-7). The dross in our sinful natures is burnt off in such afflictions.

> God has put them to the test
> and proved them worthy to be with him;
> he has tested them like gold in a furnace,
> and accepted them as a holocaust.
> When the time comes for his visitation, they will shine out;
> as sparks run through the stubble, so will they (Ws 3:5-7).

King David knew that his sins needed expiation. But he also knew that God was loving him greatly in times of affliction. He could shout out to Yahweh: "It was good for me to have to suffer, the better to learn your statutes" (Ps

119: 71). In such sufferings David could exhort his people: "Put your hope in Yahweh, be strong, let your heart be bold, put your hope in Yahweh" (Ps 27:14).

A beautiful image of the "shaping" of us by God is that of the potter and the clay:

> Like clay in the hands of the potter
> to mold as it pleases him,
> so are men in the hands of their Maker
> to reward as he judges right (Si 33:13).

FAITH OF OUR FATHERS

We find many outstanding examples of faith and trusting abandonment in the Old Testament. St. Paul (Rm 4:18-25) appeals to Abraham as the model of faith and hope in God in adversities whose *rationale* escapes our human understanding. Abraham had been promised a progeny more numerous than the stars. Yet God seemingly was asking him to put his only son to death. Abraham did not doubt what his human reason could not understand but he "drew strength from faith and gave glory to God, convinced that God had power to do what he had promised" (Rm 4:21).

The Patriarch Joseph could have doubted God's love when his brothers threw him into a well or sold him as a slave to Ismaelite merchants for twenty pieces of silver (Gn 37:28). Sitting in prison because he did not yield to the temptations offered him by Putiphar's wife, Joseph could have asked God *why*. Trial after trial led him to a loving trust in God's Providence. Thus God used him to save his people in a great famine, more importantly, to raise him up as a type of the Messiah to come—Jesus.

King David, both in his sins and in his abandonment by his friends and supporters, learned how to hope in Yahweh as the source of all strength and blessing (Ps 27:14). Yahweh spoke to him and continues to say to us if we, like David, hearken to His voice:

I rescue all who cling to me,
I protect whoever knows my name,
I answer everyone who invokes me,
I am with them when they are in trouble;
I bring them safety and honor.
I give them life, long and full,
and show them how I can save (Ps 91:14-16).

POVERTY AND RICHES

Jesus came among us as a poor man but not destitute. He saw the Father working in all events (Jn 5:17) and therefore He used and enjoyed the material creatures of this earth to glorify His Heavenly Father. He taught us that we must abandon ourselves to God in any excessive solicitude or anxiety (Mt 6:25-34; Lk 12:22-32). The reason that we can abandon ourselves trustingly to God is that "your Father well knows you need them" (Lk 12:31). We need only seek God's kingdom, letting Him have sovereign control in our lives, and then all such temporalities will be given to us.

Such abandonment can manifest itself in a variety of styles of life. St. Benedict Labre and St. Francis of Assisi surrendered to God's loving care in regard to food, clothing and shelter in a way different from an American business man, nun or housewife. All Christians are to let go of any excessive worry and trust that in the circumstances of their state of life God will provide all they need. For parents it will mean buying and keeping up a modest house, saving money for their children's education, taking out insurance against fire and theft. Abandonment and true poverty of spirit are possible in the context of using *properly* the riches God gives us.

Such trust in God gives us peace that when an economic pinch hits us we can find God in those circumstances and praise Him and trust that He will provide us with all necessities of life just as He did in more prosperous times.

It truly seems to be a contradiction that a Christian can be abandoned to God and still be excessively wealthy, beyond having a moderate income to meet his needs. What kind of Christianity do we practise if we claim to be brothers and sisters to the poor and starving and continue to be well fed and callously unconcerned about them? St. James teaches us a true Christian attitude of sharing whatever we have with the poor:

> If one of the brothers or one of the sisters is in need of clothes and has not enough food to live on, and one of you says to them, 'I wish you well; keep yourself warm and eat plenty,' without giving them these bare necessities of life, then what good is that? Faith is like that: if good works do not go with it, it is quite dead (Jm 2:15-17).

Abandonment, therefore, not only means getting rid of excessive worries to have the necessities of life but it means abandoning excessive attachments to the possessions that God has so generously given us by giving to the needy whatever is above our moderate needs. Jesus taught this concern for the poor and needy and promised that our eternal judgment would center on how we shared ourselves and our possessions with the hungry, the thirsty, the stranger, the naked, the sick, the prisoners (Mt 25:35-40).

HEALTH AND SICKNESS

Most of us have enjoyed many more years of health than of sickness. We can praise God for we know the gift that health has been. As healthy beings, we can grow in deep, personal relationships of love with others. We can work diligently in giving ourselves to others in a Christian apostolate. Health aids us to pray well, to travel and pursue many enriching human experiences. "Yahweh gave. . . . Blessed be the name of Yahweh!" (Jb 1:21).

But true abandonment in sickness can bring us to believe that the lack of health also can be a gift. "Yahweh has taken back. Blessed be the name of Yahweh!" (Jb 1:21). Most human beings suffer at some time in their life from some degree or other of sickness or disease, especially toward the end of their life. It is naive to think that all sickness is from devils. God can do anything He wishes. If He permits it to happen to us or even wills it, He is really wishing us, not sickness as an end, but rather He is wishing us greater health, a more total happiness.

We need to take reasonable care of our health. We can hardly believe that God is responsible for our sicknesses if we do not eat property, usually by over-eating excessively or eating only "junk" foods because we are too lazy to prepare wholesome food, or do not sleep sufficiently or worry excessively. But even with a moderate care of our health, sickness can come to us. Such an occasion can be a blessing if we can accept it properly in the context of God's Providence. We test our trust in God in such circumstances of weakness. When the physical powers of our body, our senses, our intellectual acumen, memory etc. begin to lessen, we have the graceful opportunity to experience our creatureliness and poverty before God. All other virtues, especially greater faith, hope and love towards God, develop if we utilize such sufferings to open to God as our sole strength.

Even when we find ourselves murmuring or losing patience, this very weakness can be a grace to cry out all the more that God come to our assistance. De Caussade writes of this in a letter:

> . . . you are to thank God, as though for a grace, for what you suffer meanly and weakly, that is to say, without much courage. At such times you feel overcome by your ills, upon the verge of giving way to them, inclined to grumble about them and to yield to the rebelliousness of your human nature. Indeed, this is a true grace and a great grace at that, since to suffer this is to suffer with humility and with no great spirit. . . . It is what Fenelon describes as becoming little in our own eyes and allowing ourselves to be humbled by a perception of our weakness in suffering. Were this truth well known to all people of goodwill, with what peace and tranquility they would suffer, knowcng neither restlessness nor any reflection of self-love on their own weakness and the lack of conscious courage with which they suffer![1]

PRAYING FOR HEALING

Is it a greater display of abandonment not to pray for the alleviation of any physical or temporal inconvenience, especially of bodily sickness? Jesus has clearly taught us to ask our Heavenly Father for "our daily bread," meaning all our temporal needs. We ask for such in conformity to God's good pleasure. Jesus tells us to ask for anything of the Father in His name (Lk 11:9-13; Jn 14:13-14; 16:23).

Not only did Jesus insist on our praying to the Father for whatever we deemed necessary in our kingdom relationships as children to our Father, but He preached the necessity of a childlike confidence and a persevering spirit in prayer. We read in the Book of Tobias how God heard the prayers of Tobias (Tb 12:8) and of young Sarah (Tb 3:24-25). The Old Testament is a continuous catalogue of persons praying and receiving a positive answer from God. "Blessed be Yahweh, for he hears the sound of my petition!" (Ps 28:6).

But for Christians of the New Covenant with Jesus as our High Priest interceding for us before the Father's throne, we can pray with confidence and perseverance. "The heartfelt prayer of a good man works very powerfully" (Jm 5:17). Like the man beseeching his neighbor at night to give him some bread for his visiting friend (Lk 11:5-8) or the importunate widow before the judge (Lk 18:1-8), we are to ask unceasingly with boldness and constancy. When we pray, we must pray as though we already have what we pray for, and it will be given as we believe (Mk 11:24).

We also do not know how to pray even to offer petitions to God as we ought. The Christian responsibility is to put on the mind of Jesus when He prays to His Father, "not my will but yours be done" (Lk 22:42). Only by praying in the Spirit of Jesus will our prayer be pleasing to God.

> The Spirit too comes to help us in our weakness. For when we cannot choose words in order to pray properly, the Spirit himself expresses our plea in a way that could never be put

into words, and God who knows everything in our hearts knows perfectly well what he means, and that the pleas of the saints expressed by the Spirit are according to the mind of God (Rm 8:26-27).

Thus in praying to the Father through the intercession of Jesus, we must first go to prayer to see just what we should pray for and how. If we, in prayer, see this or that ailment or sickness as an obstacle to God's glory working in us and a healing as contributing more to God's praise, then we pray for healing. As we pray, we enlarge our petition. We are praying for a concrete healing (and the same applies for praying for any other request: a new job, cessation of war, etc.) and as we pray we open ourselves to receive from the Holy Spirit a deeper infusion of faith, hope and love.

We pray with faith, absolutely assured that God will heal us and give us a greater health unto more total life and happiness. We pray without wavering as St. James tells us (Jm 1:6-8) because we believe God always heals. As we pray and receive the absolute answer to a healing of our unbelief, as we can let go of our fears and doubts, as the love of God pours powerfully into our spirits, we now know that we can do all things in God who strengthens us. Our very weakness and sickness become our strength and spiritual healing.

Thus from such prayer of faith, individually prayed or in a group, we can begin thanking God, not only for the healing of the spirit by deeper faith, but also for a total healing. Perhaps in this life, in the Providence of God, the increased healing is not manifested in a bodily or psychical healing. Yet the very continued presence of the sickness or suffering is now a source of greater grace, happiness and spiritual health that will enhance the body and soul healing in the life to come.

ACCEPTING ONESELF

Many serious Christians can accept great adversities from natural external causes but fail often in a balanced acceptance of themselves with all the imperfections and limitations that implies. Adrian van Kaam well describes two types who seek perfection. One projects an ideal type that he or she strives to become without, however, the slightest regard for the person he or she really is in life's existential context. The other type realistically sees what he or she is like and only too readily accepts that reality without willing to change that given personality.[2]

Abandonment to God's will is a loving, humble acceptance of the gifts that God has freely given us. He could have given us more talents, greater wisdom, an ability to sing, speak, write, heal, etc. He could have given us less. Jesus' parable of the talents bears out the mysterious gratuitousness of God's distribution of talents (Mt 25:14-30). Yet we must trustingly surrender ourselves to God, knowing that His love for each of us is unique. As star differs from star, so each of us is loved uniquely by God. If we are the result of all of our past experiences and God, in His uncreated energies, has been working in each past moment out of love for us individually, then we can easily understand how we are each a special universe of God's creation. We cannot, in pride, envy or jealousy, compare our talents with those received by others.

It is for us to be grateful to God at all times for His gifts and with His graces to develop them for His glory. Thus pride, that tempts us to be someone of power beyond the will or good-pleasure of God, is conquered by a childlike humility and loving acceptance of God's Providence. Also a laziness and pessimistic resignation are overcome by accepting God's expressed will from Holy Scripture to multiply and bring forth even greater fruit. All anxieties and fears, aggressiveness through envy and jealousy towards others and their seemingly superior gifts are eradicated from our lives as we joyfully accept our limitations and our uniqueness and praise God for His goodness in working differently in others.

By accepting ourselves and our talents we can also accept the employments given us in the Providence of God. Television has given many Americans the disquieting illusion that by merely wishing it, they can become all things. Teachers in schools find that the youth are very self-confident, ambitious for higher pursuits, high-paying jobs, yet they often do not possess the native ability or the perseverance to master basic skills through monotonous, unexciting study disciplines. Abandonment to God in our work is basically an act of humble submission to God's creative plan for us. He wants us to add some creative work to the human history as humanity moves to its completion even though in terms of the Hollywood tinsel culture it may not seem to exciting or earthshaking. Tuning in, by faith and trust, to what God is asking of us by way of work through a creative development of God's gifts, can bring us much peace, joy and love which mean great human development.

RELATIONS WITH OTHERS

One of the continued areas of abandoning ourselves to God's holy will is in our varied relationships with other human beings. Often it is the area of what Teilhard de Chardin calls *passive diminishments*. Others act upon us, loving or hating us or simply being indifferent to us. We may be willing to accept ourselves, but are we always ready to find God's Providence in the way others accept us?

We can readily accept the praises and love from friends, but can we praise God's Providence in snubs, coldness, calumnies and detractions, not only from seeming enemies, but above all from our friends and even members of our own community or family? Such negative "put-downs" of our own dignity require a deep faith and trusting abandonment to God's love in order to find good in such events.

Yet we can see intellectually how such humiliations can aid us to grow in true Christian love, in patience and gentleness, meekness and humility toward others and in great surrender to God's presence in such happenings.

The *Imitation of Christ* expresses this doctrine very well in terms of creating a sense of pilgrimage on this earth and helping us to humility by avoiding vain glory:

> It is good for us now and then to have some troubles and adversities; for often times they make a man enter into himself, that he may know that he is an exile, and place not his hopes in anything of the world. It is good for us sometimes to suffer contradictions and to allow people to think ill and slightingly of us, even when we do and mean well. These are often helps to humility, and rid us of vain glory. For then we more earnestly seek God to be witness of what passes within us, when outwardly we are slighted by men, and incur their discredit. [3]

There is no authentic hymility without humiliations. And the best humiliations are those that we need not work at by our own design but that just "happen" within the context of our daily lives. Perhaps none of us will have such humiliations to suffer as St. John of the Cross who was put into a dungeon by his own fellow religious for months with little food or drink but a constant diet of reproaches and beatings. St. Alphonsus Ligouri was expelled from the Redemptorist Congregation which he himself had founded.

SUFFERING FOR THE KINGDOM

But we do often experience coldness, sharp words, suspicions, indifference, especially from the very ones who should be returning our love. How often our very love of Christ seems to be the occasion of suffering rebukes and humiliations, even from very good people, religious superiors, the local pastor, persons with whom we normally pray together. Jesus pronounced a special blessing on such:

> Happy those who are persecuted in the cause of right: theirs is the kingdom of heaven. Happy are you when people abuse you and persecute you and speak all kinds of calumny against you on my account. Rejoice and be glad for your reward will be great in heaven; this is how they persecuted the prophets before you (Mt 5:10-12).

St. Paul also exhorts us Christians to the reality that we will be called to suffer for the sake of Jesus Christ: "You are well aware, then, that anybody who tries to live in devotion to Christ is certain to be attacked" (2 Tm 3:13).

In such circumstances the gentleness and patience, constancy and forgiveness of Jesus, the Lamb of God, silent before His shearers, should be our model and strength. In such abandonment we are really allowing Jesus and His Spirit to bring us healing of our aggressive pride and selfishness. As we lovingly and joyfully accept such adversities from others acting upon us, we begin to see them, not as crosses alone, but as steps to a new transformation into Christ. We praise God for such happenings as we grow in greater gentleness and humility. We may never *like* such sufferings, but we can experience the blessings that flow from them when we abandon ourselves to let Jesus be Lord in such occasions.

DEATH

In no physical adversity do we find more exercise of abandonment than in the face of death, our own or that of a loved one. God gives us a built-in instinct to preserve our life against any threatening, exterior forces. Added to this is our sinful nature which without faith wants to possess this life forever. Thus any dissolution of human life comes with a struggle, the terrifying death struggle to step over to the "other side." Dr. Elizabeth Kubler Ross, Dr. Karlis Osis and R. Moody have recorded in their studies of the clinically dead who have returned, resuscitated, to this life, that dying is often experienced as a joyful entrance into light, accompanied by deceased loved ones.

Still faith in a life after death and abandonment to God's infinite mercy should have their greatest exercise in that final moment. If it is a loved one whom we shall never see again in this life, our abandonment to God's Providence must conquer our natural loss. We must not go to pieces as though this person was the whole purpose of our life rather than God. The wisdom of St. Basil should be ours as we read his advice to a mother who had recently lost her little child through death:

Let the will of God cohabit with your will; like a light which penetrates everything by its rays, it will be there without interruption to bring you to pass an accurate judgment on things. Way back in advance it sees to it that your soul is protected; it prepares the true ideas concerning every event, and will not allow you to lose your bearings, whatever may happen. Your mind having previously been trained will meet with the unshakable and steady strength of a rock by the seashore the furious onslaughts of winds and surging waves.[4]

Our own death should be a culmination of many acts of abandonment to accept whatever comes to us joyfully and trustingly through God's Providence. No doubt there will be regret in all our hearts for all of us could have brought forth greater fruit with God's graces.

God alone knows and controls the time and the circumstances of our death. The Christian trusts in God's mercy and wisdom above all, in His infinite love that all things work unto our good. Faith in Jesus Christ who conquered sin and death should be so great that both in life and in death the Christian believes in the words of the Prophet Isaiah: "He will destroy Death forever. The Lord Yahweh will wipe away the tears from every cheek" (Is 25:8).

We truly die as we live. Those who have lived by deep faith, hope and love will die in such virtues. The childlike spirit of abandonment will be operative in that ultimate "letting-go." The peace and joy of the Holy Spirit that filled their earthly pilgrimage in times of adversities will flood them in abundance on their deathbed.

Such a Christian has daily said with St. Paul: "I face death everyday" (1 Co 15:31). He fears no adversity, not even death, for by daily abandoning his desires to those of God's holy will, he knows that nothing in life or death can ever separate him from the love of Christ (Rm 8:38). All through his earthly life but climaxed in final death, he experiences a blessed security and certitude, not in his own power or merits from good works, but in God's infinite love for him. In life and in death, while still in the corruptible body, he already experiences something of immortality, incorruptibility, the unchangeability of God's eternal love for him.

Death, therefore, has no sting, no victory over him because he has died to sin and now lives in the victory of Jesus Christ (1 Co 15:54-57). Thus in the face of death he fears nothing, for his strength is in his Risen Savior.

> But we believe that having died with Christ we shall return to life with him. Christ, as we know, having been raised from the dead will never die again. Death has no power over him any more. When he died, he died, once for all, to sin, so his life now is life with God; and in that way, you too must consider yourselves to be dead to sin but alive for God in Christ Jesus (Rm 6:8-11).

Abandonment to God by submitting oneself to the kingship of Jesus Christ is the answer that the Christian Job gives to the world's dilemma about suffering and final death. Abandonment to seek the good-pleasure of God in all circumstances of our earthly life is a constant death to ourselves, but also a continuously realized resurrection into the Risen Body of Jesus. No evil can touch one who *nests in the Rock* that is Jesus Christ.

9

Abandonment in Contemplation

One of the great phenomena of the 1970's has been the hunger on the part of a great many people of all ages and of all walks of life to meet God deeply, inwardly in a greater awareness of His indwelling and dynamically loving presence. *Mysticism* is not a fad. Karl Rahner insists: "The devout Christian of the future will either be a 'mystic,' one who has 'experienced' something, or he will cease to be anything at all."[1]

Any Christian who is not only to survive as a Christian but above all to grow must progressively move away from an immature clinging exclusively to external forms in religion. He must grow in great awareness that God is a Person, a loving Father, who is acting constantly in every moment of his life.

No doubt our Western materialism, extreme activism with little time for silent reflection and solitude and a gross conformity to *fadism* have hastened this hunger for inwardness. Western man cries out desperately to meet again the living God of Abraham, Isaac and Jacob, not in dry concepts, but in a personal encounter between an *I* and a *Thou*.

It is, therefore, inwardly that you are to go to find your true freedom. Beyond all pre-conditionings of your false self, your past training, thought patterns, even sins, you enter deeper and deeper, down into the depths of your consciousness that pushes to claim new areas of conquest in the dark recesses of the unconscious. You push in prayerful encounter with God through the various strata of your emotions, affections, beyond the confinement of fixity arranged comfortably into a *status quo* through heredity and the social relationships of your past life.

All of this is a part of yourself, but not quite your *true* self. There is so much more of you to come into being if you had the courage to enter into the interior battle. God is calling you constantly into a process of letting go of the controlled activity you have been exercising in your prayer life. You stand on the fringe of the barren desert. You have met and known God in vocal and meditative prayer. There was a need to meet the objective God as He has appeared in the history of salvation in the prophetic words of Holy Scripture.

MEDITATIVE PRAYER

Most Christians begin to know God by means of a disciplined form of discursive prayer. This usually consists in taking a page from Scripture, a scene from the Old or New Testament. We go through it, reading it slowly, pondering its meaning. With our imagination, memory, understanding and will we arrive at some affective "presence" to God. Our faith, trust and love grow slowly over months and years of such meditation.

As the Holy Spirit infuses these gifts into our hearts, we are able to move from the given text to the presence of

God and His divine action. The things, especially, that Jesus said and did, as recorded in the New Testament, become experienced in this moment of prayer. The *where* or the *when* are no longer so important as we enter into the process of letting go of our own control of this historical moment (*chronos*) to encounter the saving Lord who transcends the limitations of all time and place.

As your act of faith brings you progressively more and more deeply into the presence of Jesus Christ, His resurrectional presence begins to work upon you. You meet the only Christ alive today in the event of His person living within you.

A PEACEFUL PRESENCE

As you move into this simple presence of Jesus Christ, there is a great peace and quietude. Often intense affections surge up with ardent longings to be more intimately united with Him and the Heavenly Father. The consolations in this period of your prayer life can be strong and attractive. God seems to be everywhere, even outside of your period of concentrated prayer along with God. A global presence of Jesus Christ surrounds you and you begin to find Him in the world around you, in places and persons where you had never "seen" Him before.

You begin to yield with greater susceptibility to His loving presence. Your aggressive activity both in prayer and in your daily actions takes on a gentleness and docility to the indwelling presence of God, both within yourself and within all of creation around you. There is a "letting go" of your power and a new sensitivity, a new listening to God's presence and loving activity around you. You seem to be living on a new plateau of awareness of God's presence.

Whether there is ardent consolation or just dryness, there seems to be a deep peace and joy that events which, formerly were disturbing, now do not seem to destroy.

Through the years of meditating on the prophetic words in Scripture, you now have a facility of listening to the existential Word, Jesus Christ, God's Speech, talking to you in the storm that bursts upon you, in the suffering old man before your eyes, the laughing child in play, the traumatic earthquake destroying hundreds and thousands of human lives of your fellow brothers and sisters in a foreign land. You now find that it is God's activity that you are able to perceive and always in the light of a deepening faith that you are loved greatly by Jesus Christ and His Father. There is a sense of growing unity with God and with the world. Anxieties of the moment are surrendered in a childlike trust in God's presence in this or that moment.

PURIFYING DARKNESS

But the sensible presence of God soon passes. As you continue walking along the paths of prayer, eager for greater union with God, you find no longer that sweet presence of God. It is as if you lost Him. The Song of Songs describes your experience in prayer:

On my bed, at night, I sought him
whom my heart loves.
I sought but did not find him. . . .
I will seek him whom my heart loves.
. . . I sought but did not find him.
The watchmen came upon me
on their rounds in the City:
'Have you seen him whom my heart loves?' (Sg 3:1-3).

A new presence of God indwelling within you shows itself as darkness. The more that you discover God as loving Father, the farther God seems away. You have a dull sense of alienation as you seem to enter deeply within yourself. You see your own abyss of nothingness before the mountain of God's majesty. There is a feeling of self-dread with a crying out in urgency for the face of God. Faith is deepening without the props of sensible consolation, images, words. The more you advance into this darkness, the more names about God and His attributes have no sense. Nothing satisfies you. The very presence of God that had flooded you both in deep affective prayer and in contact with the world now seems utterly absent.

God creates this necessary pruning, this dying of the seed in order that greater union with Him is possible. You enter into a necessary dying to your self-reliance and a deepening of faith that only come when you are in this darkness, standing before a wall that is impermeable by your own intellectual powers.

It is a crying out for God to show Himself in the night of the desert, where you understand your own absolute nothingness before God. There is a silencing of your own powers like the silence of steel in the black night. Only a person who has experienced this trial can understand because God has been all to this person. And now you have to dig roots and cry out in deep, dark, stark faith for the mercy of God: "Lord, Jesus Christ, have mercy on me!"

MOVING TO CONTEMPLATION

St. John of the Cross, the great teacher of contemplative prayer, gives us concrete signs whereby we can discern when a person moves from a discursive, meditative type of prayer into a greater simplification of faith, the beginning of the life of contemplation and the call to a greater abandonment to God in such faith. It is worth quoting him in full as to these signs in order to discern a true movement of the Spirit and a call to authentic contemplation that is quite different from tepidity and sloth in prayer.

> The first is the realization that one cannot make discursive meditation nor receive satisfaction from it as before. Dryness is now the outcome of fixing the senses upon subjects which formerly provided satisfaction. As long as one can, however, make discursive meditation and draw out satisfaction, one must not abandon this method. Meditation must only be discontinued when the soul is placed in that peace and quietude to be spoken of in the third sign.

> The second sign is an awareness of a disinclination to fix the imagination or sense faculties upon other particular objects, exterior or interior. I am not affirming that the imagination will cease to come and go (even in deep recollection it usually wanders freely), but that the person is disinclined to fix it purposely upon extraneous things.

> The third and surest sign is that a person likes to remain alone in loving awareness of God, without particular considerations, in interior peace and quiet and repose, and without the acts and exercises (at least discursive, those in which one progresses from point to point) of the intellect, memory and will; and that he prefers to remain only in the general, loving awareness and knowledge we mentioned, without any particular knowledge or understanding.

> To leave safely the state of meditation and sense and enter that of contemplation and spirit, the spiritual person must observe within himself at least these three signs together.[2]

One should remember that, as one does not abandon oneself completely to God in a given moment and it remains a fixed state of abandonment for the rest of one's life, so entering into the state of contemplation and the way of purer faith does not happen in one given moment, never to return to meditation. At times meditation will be possible and even desirable. At other times reading a few prayers at the beginning to "localize" oneself before God's majesty may be helpful. The use of the Jesus Prayer can be an excellent means of centering oneself deeply in the presence of the Trinity and thus putting oneself into a "faithful" presence of God.

You may have doubts in such a simplified prayer that you are really praying. There are few concrete acts to fall back upon to give you certitude that you are accomplishing anything or that you really are praying. Yet your activity consists now in pushing your will to become more united with that of God, even though there may be extreme dryness and even harmless distractions that cannot be avoided. It is to be expected that as you stop using your discursive powers of intellect, will and imagination that there will be much wandering of these faculties in search for images and ideas upon which to feed.

Thus such a prayer of faith has a negative element of slowing down the use of these faculties. A definite purgation process takes place. Even though the thought of God does not necessarily bring any consolation, faith is being exercised in a new way, freed from any ideas or words. The most evident purgation takes place in what St. John of the Cross describes as: "Since God puts a soul in this dark night in order to dry up and purge its sensory appetite, He does not allow it to find sweetness or delight in anything."[3]

We must actively intensify our activities and reflection on our daily living to check whether there is any sinful attachment or imperfections that are possibly at the root of such dryness. Abandonment to God in contemplation avoids the errors of Quietism that so sickly gave up all activity on the part of the contemplative, especially in the area of self-examination. Such erroneous teaching held that true abandonment meant the abandonment of all self-activity and that sinful actions committed in such a state of deep, faithful abandonment would not be true sins.

The true apophatic theology of the Eastern Fathers is best expressed in the classical work of Pseudo-Dionysius who describes the knowing by unknowing:

> . . . and then It (God's presence in darkness) breaks forth, even from the things that are beheld and from those that behold them, and plunges the true initiate into the Darkness of Unknowing wherein he renounces all the apprehensions of his understanding and is enwrapped in that which is wholly intangible and invisible, belonging wholly to Him that is beyond all things and to none else (whether himself or another), and being through the passive stillness of all his reasoning powers united by his highest faculty to Him that is wholly Unknowable, of whom thus by a rejection of all knowledge he possesses a knowledge that exceeds his understanding. [4]

POSITIVE ASPECT

The positive aspect in contemplative faith is an inexplicable sense of the presence of God, even though on the level of discursive powers He seems absent. Tyis is the operation of faith of the Holy Spirit giving you a new interior sense of "seeing" God. Leonard Boase describes this as a "sixth sense":

It is a communion with God in which the soul is aware of His reality and of His presence by a sort of 'six-sense' or 'second-sight' or 'telepathy' which is specifically different from the kind of certainty that He exists attained by logical demonstration. It is a certainty different also from the assent of faith given by Christians in every day conditions; but it differs from this not specifically, but only because that same certainty of faith has moved, so to speak, into the sensitive focus of consciousness. [5]

Writers speak of the "ligature" of the senses, a letting-go process of such sense-knowledge acquired principally by our own activities. This state of prayer of faith is different from an earlier state of affections through the use of aspirations during the period of prayer or during one's activities. In this state you abandon yourself to the presence of affections and consolations. Great peace and joy come over you during the entire day, even though in given periods of concentrated attention to God there is also great aridity. This type of peace has nothing to do with a false peace of tepid satisfaction with one's present state of being. True peace in this stage of abandonment in contemplation is rooted in our own dissatisfaction of ourselves, our sinful darkness that we have now found lying below the surface of our habitual consciousness. Along with that dissatisfaction the increase of faith and abandonment to God's loving presence mounts to a new pitch that far exceeds the sense of God's presence earlier experienced in affective prayer.

Totally surrendered to God, we live only for Him as each moment brings us an occasion to be a living gift back to God. A new threshold of union with God has been reached that has passed through the dread of the purification of the senses. God has taken away from us all attachment to sense pleasures. Nothing or no one can be now the source of any attraction without a conscious submission of that relationship to God's holy will.

Hugh of St. Victor has well described this state of union with God where God comes and goes, yet always remains. Only He is loved by the contemplative.

Yes, it is truly the Beloved who visits thee. But He comes invisible, hidden, incomprehensible. He comes to touch thee, not to be seen; to intimate His presence to thee, not to be understood; to make thee taste of Him, not to pour Himself out in His entirety; to draw thy affection, not to satisfy thy desire; to bestow the first-fruits of His love, not to communicate it in its fulness. Behold in this the most certain pledge of thy future marriage: that thou art destined to see Him and to possess Him eternally, because He already gives Himself to thee at times to taste; with what sweetness thou knowest. Therefore, in the times of His absence thou shalt console thyself; and during His visits thou shalt renew thy courage which is ever in need of heartening. We have spoken at great length, O my soul, I ask thee to think of none but Him, love none but Him, listen to none but Him, to take hold of none but Him, possess none but Him.[6]

You move onto a new level of praising God, not because He is good to you, but an increase in hope now allows you to praise Him in every event, whether it be pleasing to self or unpleasant, whether in prayer you be found in consolation or desolation. In all things you praise Him because you desire to do so because God is desired, not for what He can do for you, but sheerly because He is goodness in Himself and infinitely loving.

A DIAPHANOUS WORLD

The whole world now becomes a diaphanous presence of God's love, shining through to you. No longer do you find a world that is somehow sacred and a different world that is profane. You move, not as an angel ignoring this world around you, but rather you see now the world in all its uniqueness and yet precisely that uniqueness is discovered in the finality of God's creative love.

You have entered into true freedom. No longer do you see blindly merely in the light of your own world built up by your desires and projections. You have died to yourself and now you are alive to Jesus Christ. You live according to the Father's Logos found in each situation. You see Christ everywhere. It is already a share in the vision that will be face-to-face in Heaven, but the substance is already encountered of God's immense love in each moment made manifest through His Word-Incarnate, Jesus Christ. The world is now being transfigured by the presence and power of God in all things. You realize now that you are called by Him to be a reconciler of the whole world, as St. Paul writes (2 Co 5:18). Earth is already full of God's glory and you are privileged to see part of it, depending on the purification that you submit to, the dying to self.

Such a purified contemplative is gifted by a new faith and hope and love to discover God at the core of each person encountered. A reverence sweeps over you as you open to the God in each human being, as you abandon yourself to serve that godly presence. Now just as in deep contemplation, so in life's situations there is no optimal event desired by you in which God can more perfectly reveal Himself. Through your purified faith you can see the hand of God, loving you with the same type of love and creativity in each and every moment.

THE NIGHT OF THE SPIRIT

Despite the earlier purgation of the senses that saw the abandonment of yourself in deeper faith to give up any discursive meditation, based on sense knowledge and a great deal of your own activity, you are in need of still greater purification. The intellect and will begin to experience intense aridities, darkness and interior conflicts. God is perfecting His work of purifying His chosen children. This is a call to put away the mentality of an immature child as St. Paul exhorts us: "When I was a child, I used to talk like a child, and think like a child, and argue like a child, but now I am a man, all childish ways are put behind me" (1 Co 13:11). God actively enters into the purifying process. Even though He uses the sins and failures of others, He also actively begins a process of stripping the old man in order that, as St. Paul says, the new man can be brought forth. St. John of the Cross describes this process and gives the reason for it:

> . . . God divests the faculties, affections and senses, both spiritual and sensory, interior and exterior. He leaves the intellect in darkness, the will in aridity, the memory in emptiness and the affections in supreme affliction, bitterness, and anguish, by depriving the soul of the feeling and satisfaction it previously obtained from spiritual blessings. For this privation is one of the conditions required that the spiritual form, which is the union of love, may be introduced in the spirit and united with it. The Lord

works all of this in the soul by means of a pure and dark contemplation . . .[7]

God humbles us and completes our detachment in our intellectual and volitional faculties. God wants to draw us into a deeper union and more intense knowledge that is His pure gift. Everything of self must, therefore, disappear as we are made to realize our own nothingness and utter weakness. In such darkness you will learn how to let go the last hold you have on your own controlled knowledge and ideas about God. It becomes impossible for you to think discursively. Spiritual reading and prayer become a heavy burden.

I have described this darkness and purification of the spirit:

The night seems very dense and dark, the desert seems very dry and empty. One feels that he will never find God again; and yet there is no true panic or disquietude. There is only a deep abiding trust that God will come; that in a way He is present in His absence. The soul is being called to experience God in a new modality, no longer experiencing Him through one's own concepts or feelings with assuring repercussions in one's physical life, but now nakedly through faith. Faith grows as we come to know God in the unknowable. The soul feels immobile, blocked at the bottom of the mountain, completely alone, crying out to God for His infinite mercy. God is so much the Other. We begin to experience our creatureliness, our poverty and our utter dependence upon God. To become a true contemplative, to let God do with us what He wants, demands the greatest suffering.[8]

The darkness that invades the mind fills you with

repugnance, disgust and an interior revolt. The revolt is registered in the lower part of your consciousness, something like that felt by Jesus in the Garden of Gethsemane (Lk 22:42). You have the impression that you can do nothing, that you are totally deprived of any power to extricate yourself from the darkness. Still in your higher powers, of intellect and will, permeated by a purer faith, a more complete hope, you are able to push your consciousness to a purified love of God. You push on in surrendering yourself to the free operation of God's grace in your spiritual life. With no sensible fervor felt and a deep awareness of your own weaknesses, failings and limitations, you enter into an interior battle of fresh and violent temptations that add to the growing conviction that you have fallen from fidelity to God.

To stay in the battle and seek to be faithful, to seek light and a way out of the turmoil, only heighten the anguish felt. And yet patience and fortitude must be exercised. It is here that one's abandonment to God in such interior trials must be also manifested in perfect obedience and trust to one's spiritual director. Hopefully such a spiritual director will be enlightened both from his own experience in advanced contemplation and from his study of mystical theology and the writings of the great Christian mystics not to insist that such trials are the result of sin or necessarily from other natural causes, laziness, tepidity and melancholy. Too often a spiritual director can add to the trials unnecessarily by his lack of experience and knowledge by insisting that the contemplative hasten back to a level of prayer that is more controlled and more certain. Too often such directors do not move with the Holy Spirit to respect the workings of God in the individual needs of the directee.

Again, to quote from the sound teaching of St. John of the Cross:

> And a little of this that God works in the soul in this holy idleness and solitude is an inestimable good, a good much greater at times than a person or his director can imagine. And although one is not always so clearly conscious of it, it will in due time shed its light. The least that a person can manage to feel is a withdrawal and an estrangement as to all things, sometimes more than at other times, accompanied by an inclination toward solitude and a weariness with all creatures and with the world, in the gentle breathing of love and life in the spirit. [9]

The value of such a purification is that it brings the purification of the senses and the intellectual faculties into a oneness with a more total surrender now to the sovereignty of God.

PRAY FOR CONSOLATIONS

Should you pray for consolations after you have been tried for some time? St. Ignatius in his *Spiritual Exercises* tells the retreatant to remember the times he was in consolation and to be strengthened by that thought. One can also pray to be delivered from temptations as we are taught by Jesus Himself in the Our Father, "Lead us not into temptation, but deliver us from evil." The great danger at this stage of your spiritual development is that you will lose patience and courage. Your abandonment to God's holy will reaches so far and you wish now to take things into your hands. If you have prayed earnestly for relief and have found that the trials and temptations continue, you can recognize that God is permitting it by not answering your prayer as you wish, in a similar manner that Jesus prayed to have the chalice of suffering pass Him by in Gethsemane, yet He continued to surrender Himself all the more in the higher level of His will to accept lovingly His Father's will.

Deep abandonment comes in stifling and repelling the desire to be free from such sufferings and abandoning yourself completely to accept whatever the good Lord sends you even if it should be greater suffering. You should focus in such abandonment on the prayer to obtain grace to accept joyfully and with courage whatever God wishes to send. Such a prayer will always be granted since God never tempts us beyond our strength. St. Paul writes: "You can trust God not to let you be tried beyond your strength, and with any trial he will give you a way out of it and the strength to bear it" (1 Co 10:13).

Thus you grow daily in the conviction that is beyond your reasoning but that comes to you in your broken state through the infusion of deeper faith, hope and love by the Holy Spirit who gives His graces to the humble. If you believe sincerely that nothing can happen to you except by God's will, and if you have no other desire but to be actively doing God's will, it is self-evident that no matter what happens to you, you will always have only what you desire. Your will is now completely one with God's. Such trials become a saving cross and give God great glory when you accept them in loving union with Him.

FEAR AND SCRUPULOSITY

One of the great results of such trials and temptations is the infusion into the humble, purified person a deeper sense of reverence for God and fear of self. No external humiliation can bring about a sense of creatureliness and humility as such interior purifications of the spirit, when endured patiently over a long period of time, if such be God's permissive or deliberative will.

But accompanying such fear, especially for a certain type of interior person, can be a severe temptation of scruples. Scrupulosity can never be from God for it cloaks a subtle temptation to pride and a complete lack of trust in God's mercy. It is one of the worst trials that one can undergo in the spiritual life which renders prayer inefacacious due to a self-absorption that cannot be pleasing to God. It does not spring from a delicacy of conscience and a desire to please God, but rather from an ignorance, error or defective judgment. Usually such a person refuses to obey both his or her spiritual director and the common teaching of the Church in such a matter.

There is no distinction between imperfection and true sinfulness. The awful judgment of God is accentuated with little trust in His infinite love and mercy. Slightest faults will be magnified to gigantic crimes. The conscience becomes raw and tenderized like bare feet that walk for miles over stony roads. Such a person cannot be his own judge and must submit to the prudent judgment of his confessor or director. Such a person usually has inherited a melancholic disposition or is extremely suspicious in nature. Scrupulosity, therefore, is a subtle form of self-love or spiritual absorption of oneself.

Still even such a state can be used by God as has happened in the lives of many great saints at various times of their lives, to bring the person of deeper prayer into a deeper abandonment and trust. The words of Dom Vital Lehodey are balanced in this matter:

God will never be directly the author of scrupulosity. It can only come from our fallen nature or from the demon, since it is founded on error and is a real malady of the soul. But He permits it; He even employs it occasionally as a *transient* means of sanctification; and in this case, He controls and directs it with His infinite wisdom, in such a manner as to make us derive from it the spiritual advantage which He has in view. He inspires the soul with a great fear of sin, in order that she may rid herself more completely of her past transgressions, and by redoubling her zeal prevent a relapse. He humbles her so that she may no longer venture to rely on her own judgment, but submit herself entirely to her spiritual father. If there is question of a soul already well advanced, He uses scrupulosity to complete her purification, her detachment, her annihilation, so as to prepare her for the reception of very special graces.[10]

THE DARK NIGHT—MAN'S REINTEGRATION

The Dark Night is the highest point before transformation and union take place in mystical prayer and is the purification that brings about man's reintegration. The contemplative must surrender to God's complete control on all levels of his being, both of the senses and in his rational self-directing. He enters into a void, an emptiness of all that may impede him from being totally surrendered to God's Spirit of love. Pure faith allows such a Christian to advance in union with God, not clinging to any knowledge derived by his own reasoning. The words of the Prophet Isaiah are especially meaningful for such a contemplative:

Let anyone who fears Yahweh among you
listen to the voice of his servant!
Whoever walks in darkness,

and has no light shining for him,
let him trust in the name of Yahweh,
let him lean on his God (Is 50:10).

The Greek Fathers, like St. Gregory of Nyssa, see the reintegration of man as a return to his connatural self. He is brought through the purifications of the dark night into a state of being "according to the image and likeness," that is Jesus Christ. St. Gregory uses the example of an icon, a painted image. Such are all of us, at birth and in God's eternal plan. We have been given deep down within us this imageness and likeness to Jesus Christ. But through heredity and faulty education, failures and sins, layers and layers of psychical and spiritual obstacles have accumulated to obscure the real image. Purifications have removed the obstacles and now the imageness that was always there is brought into all of its brilliant beauty.[11]

Now the removal of what is foreign is a return to what is connatural and fitting; and this we can only achieve by becoming what we once were in the beginning when we were created. Yet to achieve this likeness to God is not within our power nor within any human capacity. It is a gift of God's bounty, for He directly bestowed this divine likeness on our human nature at its creation.[12]

Man has returned to his true state, to a consciousness of being *in Christ* and through love to live now according to that dignity in all of his human relationships. Yet it is not a static condition but a dynamic process of continued purification and dying to selfishness and a rising to a more intense conscious relationship to God. A state of harmony is attained, bringing peace and *apatheia*, a tranquillity and

absence at the same time of any inordinate desires out of
the one great desire of loving God more intensely.

Love is the consuming fire now that burns in the heart
of the contemplative. No mystic has better captured that
state of transforming union in love than St. John of the
Cross:

O living flame of love
That tenderly wounds my soul
In its deepest center! Since
Now You are not oppressive,
Now Consummate! if it be Your will:
Tear through the veil of this sweet encounter!

O sweet cautery,
O delightful wound!
O gentle hand! O delicate touch
That tastes of eternal life
And pays every debt!
In killing You changed death to life.

O lamps of fire!
In whose splendors
The deep caverns of feeling,
Once obscure and blind,
Now give forth, so rarely, so exquisitely,
Both warmth and light to their Beloved.

How gently and lovingly
You wake in my heart,
Where in secret You dwell alone;
And in Your sweet breathing,
Filled with good and glory,
How tenderly You swell my heart with love.[13]

After such purifications the contemplative reaches a
realm of pure faith, hope and love, a state of "luminous

darkness" in which man "sees" God and is assimilated to Him in a union of wills. As God reveals Himself to the contemplative through a faith that ever grows deeper, the powers of the soul expand and "stretch forth" towards God as man's only desire. As the contemplative approaches God through contemplation, he is filled with an increase of God's uncreated energies, assimilating him into a unity with God, the Trinity, that no event can ever dissolve. Yet life's situations continuously present new possibilities of self-surrender. There is peace and joy in the transforming union already experienced. There is a burning desire still more to possess the "absent" God by a stretching out in a willed-desire to surrender oneself more completely, to suffer even more for love of God.

Thus the spiritual life based on abandonment is never a static state but a continued transformation into a progressively greater likeness to Jesus Christ.

The life of abandonment is the end of our human existence. We enter through purification and a letting go process of all our own activity to be placed by the power of the Holy Spirit in love under the guiding will of God. This is man's greatest dignity, the end for which he was created. St. Gregory fittingly gives us a close to this chapter on contemplation in his words:

> Man surpasses his own very nature. From a mortal being he becomes immortal, from a perishable being he becomes imperishable. From ephemeral he becomes eternal. In a word, from man he becomes god. In fact, rendered worthy to become a son of God, he will have in himself the dignity of the Father, enriched by all the inheritance of the goods of the Father. O munificence of the Lord, so bountiful. . . . How great are the gifts of such ineffable treasures![14]

EPILOGUE

This has been, in a way, a book about human freedom. Its basic thesis has been: those who surrender totally in each moment to the loving activities of God are the most free; indeed they are the only human beings who are really free.

Much is being written about freedom and liberation theology, yet underprivileged and oppressed people can be lifted up through long-awaited justice to a better share in the goods of the earth and still be shackled by an interior bondage. Prisoners can be freed from prisons and jails and yet they, too, can carry their prisons within themselves. Americans preach freedom to the Soviets and the Chinese and yet, how many Americans, enslaved by materialism and constant desires for more pleasures, are really free?

Jesus came on this earth to set us free:

If you make my word your home
you will indeed be my disciples,
you will learn the truth
and the truth will make you free.
. . . I tell you most solemnly,
everyone who commits sin is a slave.
Now the slave's place in the house is not assured,
but the son's place is assured.
So if the Son makes you free,
you will be free indeed. . . .

but you, you put into action
the lessons learnt from your father (Jn 8:31-38).

Freedom is not something man alone can bring about. In fact, he is born into blindness and spends a great deal of his life thinking he is his own master and therefore a slave to no one. Yet he is a victim of a power within him that drives him still further into darkness and non-reality.

Freedom is a gift that God gives man when he is ready to surrender his will to do that of God's. But one cannot know God's will except through God's revealed Word, Jesus Christ, the God-Man. He has given us much about God's will in the New Testament and in the fulfillment of the Old Testament in Him. Still He is sending us His Comforter, the Holy Spirit, so that we can become divinized as God's children by grace.

The Spirit leads us out of the darkness of anonymity into a living experience of being God's children, loved infinitely at all times by Him. The Spirit actuates within us the seeds of divine sonship that were placed within us when God created us in the image and likeness of His Divine Son. St. Macarius in his *Spiritual Homilies* captures the essential dignity of man:

> Great is the dignity of man. See how mighty are the heaven and earth, the sun and the moon; but the Lord was not pleased to rest in them but in man only. Man, therefore, is of more value than all created things — I may venture to say, not only than visible creatures, but invisible likewise, even than the ministering spirits. It was not of Michael and Gabriel, the archangels that He said, 'Let us make them after our own image and likeness, but about the spiritual substance of man.'

. . . Behold then thy dignity and of how great value thou
art, that God has made thee above the angels, because for
thy help and deliverance He came upon earth Himself in
person.[1]

Only the Son enjoys perfect freedom because at all
times He takes His whole being in hand and returns it to the
Father in loving submission. Jesus makes it possible by His
Spirit that we can enter into union with Him and with His
loving abandonment, we can live each moment in Him
toward the Father. This is, in substance, what we are
praying for in the *Our Father*: that we may do the will of the
Father on earth as it is done by the Son in Heaven. God
alone can give us, through His Son Jesus, all that we need
so as not to enter into temptation and to be delivered from
all evil.

True human freedom is grounded upon God's grace.
But as the Greek Fathers conceived grace, God in His
loving relationships is constantly surrounding us, breaking-
in upon us with His "uncreated energies." When we
consciously surrender to His loving presence, we move into
the spiritual realm, called by Jesus, the Kingdom of
Heaven. Through a conversion, a "metanoia," we turn our
"hearts" to God. We give up the "carnal" way, as St. Paul
describes it, of looking at ourselves, at God, at others and
the world around us.

God's Word becomes alive through the Father who
speaks Him in our hearts through the Holy Spirit. The
Book of Hebrews shows how God's Spirit separates our
false way of understanding from God's way:

The word of God is something alive and active: it cuts like
any double-edged sword but more finely: it can slip through

the place where the soul is divided from the spirit, or joints from the marrow; it can judge the secret emotions and thoughts. No created thing can hide from him; everything is uncovered and open to the eyes of the one to whom we must give account of ourselves (Heb 4:12-13).

God's Word in Scripture and living within us puts us in touch with God's mind. His truth begins to set us free. We have pointed out, however, the need of the desert conditions within our hearts if we are to listen attentively and with full sincerity, with "purity of heart." Although most of us living in modern cities cannot run literally into the desert as the early Christians of the fourth century did, nevertheless God's Word calls us to enter into the arid spaces, the wild, fierce darknesses within our inner world, our psychic levels of both our consciousness and unconscious and there to allow Jesus Christ to heal us and give us a new mind.

Think of God's mercy, my brothers, and worship him, I beg you, in a way that is worthy of thinking beings, by offering your living bodies as a holy sacrifice, truly pleasing to God. Do not model yourselves on the behavior of the world around you, but let your behavior change, modelled by your new mind. This is the only way to discover the will of God and know what is good, what it is that God wants, what is the perfect thing to do (Rm 12:1-2).

The desert movement is an impetus of the Holy Spirit that drives us, as He drove Jesus literally into the desert, into our deeper selves. He pushes us to go beyond the superficially controlled levels of consciousness where we distort reality by hiding behind rituals, theological formulas, "busyness" for God and neighbor. We become very adept at putting off this desert experience. Even though the Spirit knocks at the door of our heart in every event of each day (Rv 3:20), still, as Julian Green writes succinctly: "God is dying of coldness. He knocks on all the doors, but whoever opens? The room is taken. By whom? By ourselves."[2]

But one day the Spirit knocks and we temerariously at first open. Something has been eating at us. A sense of dissatisfaction, of incompleteness, of wasted life and emptiness arises from deep within us. This is mingled with a sense of being called to something higher, more transcendent. We feel powers crying out from within us to be realized. It is the inner, latent force of a spiritual spring after a long, dull, dead winter ready to burst into a rich, verdant life of beauty, color, fruit.

Are we ready to go farther into that desert and let go? Shall we hang around the oasis on the outskirts where we can still have the comforts of knowing we are "safe"? We take the first step to a new knowledge in deeper faith. We cry out with St. John of the Cross:

Reveal Your presence,
And may the vision of Your beauty be my death;
For the sickness of love
Is not cured
Except by Your very presence and image.[3]

In inner stillness, if we have the continued courage to be alone with God without our own "doing," when we have learned to "let go" of our own control over our lives, little by little artificiality crumbles. God does communicate His Word to us on a new level that is beyond words and images.

We begin to experience His awesome holiness at the depths
of our innermost being, as Moses did at the burning bush.
Our defenses fall apart and we stand stripped down to our
utter creatureliness before God our Maker. In such silence
we see the dry skeletons that we thought were a sign of our
true, living self. We cry out that God's Spirit breathe upon
them and heal them, bringing those chaotic experiences of
past years into a new life. "Lazarus, come forth!"

THE HOPE OF ABRAHAM

Man needs always to stretch out in hope towards
something beyond him, that is transcendent. Having found
that, of himself, he is not his own source of "beyondness"
and transcendence, he begins to find it in the living God of
Abraham, Isaac and Jacob and he enters into a new-
founded state of hope in God. In the midst of the ruins of
his own house, created by his own hands, hope in God is
born. Now He must be the Architect. Hope admits of many
degrees. But Abraham gives us an example in the Old
Testament of a hope that becomes actual when he learns to
let go and trusts unconditionally in God sheerly because he
believes God will be faithful to His promises.

What is impossible to man now becomes possible in
Abraham's hope. The Word of Yahweh had given him a
promise and then gave him a call to respond. Let go of your
own controlled knowledge of how your life should be run,
how God's promise will be effected, and let God take over,
simply because you trust in God's fidelity. That is the
essence of a faith like that of Abraham's.

It is such a faith, a total commitment and complete
surrender to God that leads us through the Holy Spirit into

an inner transformation that lives now only to return love for love. St. Paul prays the prayer that now should be ours:

> Out of his infinite glory, may he give you the power through his Spirit for your hidden self to grow strong, so that Christ may live in your hearts through faith, and then, planted in love and built on love, you will with all the saints have strength to grasp the breadth and the length, the height and the depth, until, knowing the love of Christ, which is beyond all knowledge, you are filled with the utter fullness of God (Eph 3:16-19).

Such an inner transformation is a process of steady dying to self in the midst of trials and conflicts that come to us from daily living. Our faith and love for God must be tested as gold is by fire (1 P 1-7). Such conflict pushes our faith, hope and love to new degrees of self-surrender.

GOD LIVES WITHIN MAN

Abandonment to God, as we have insisted on several times already, admits of many degrees. True abandonment, I believe, is an authentic index of the stage of inner freedom attained by cooperating with the Holy Spirit and of the degree of mystical union that one has reached with the indwelling Trinity.

We empty our hearts of all attachments for creatures to the degree that we discover first our own true inner self, made according to God's image. But the Spirit moves us even beyond our inner self to the indwelling Trinity. We never stop at our inner being, but that which constitutes the point of meeting God leads us to the indwelling God. It is a mirror in which we see God. It is distinct from God, yet it reflects the light and seems to be light also.

Deeper abandonment is possible by experiencing constantly the light of God within us. God's presence as light transforms us into light.

Macarius, the first great Christian mystic that spoke of mystical union in terms of God's light transforming the mystic into light, describes how man becomes all spiritual eyes of light:

> The soul that has been deemed worthy by the Spirit to participate in His light and that has been illumined by the splendor of His ineffable glory, when He has prepared it to become the throne of His glory, becomes whole light, wholly face, wholly eyes, and there remains no further part of itself that is not filled with the spiritual eyes of light. That is to say, it has nothing of darkness, but it is wholly light and spirit, wholly full of eyes, having now no back, but presenting its face on all sides, the ineffable beauty of the glory of the light of Christ having come into it and dwelling in it. Just as the sun is wholly like itself, having no other side, no inferiority, but is wholly resplendent with light, is wholly light and equally so in all its parts, or as in the fire, the light of the fire is wholly like itself, having nothing primary or secondary, greater or smaller, so the soul that has been fully illuminated by the ineffable beauty of the glory of the light of the face of Christ and filled with the Holy Spirit, worthy to become the dwelling and the temple of God, is wholly eye, wholly light, wholly face, wholly glory and wholly spirit, Christ in this way adorning it, carrying it, directing it, sustaining it and leading it and so illuminating it and decorating it with spiritual beauty.[4]

Faith and hope merge in a growing surrender to accept the light of Christ which then gives the Christian the strength to regard all other creatures as darkness or non-reality. They assume a meaningfulness only as the Christian sees them in relation to the Word of God.

Jesus Christ lives and operates within the Christian, showing Himself as an inner light in which one sees all events and all creatures. It becomes an intuitive grasp of seeing all things in Him. His light shines day and night within the heart of the contemplative of true prayer, enlightening the intelligence with a new knowledge that can never be understood by man's "natural" understanding. Christ as light is seen, not in a sensible way, but in an intelligible manner through contemplation. It is a light devoid of any form or image. This light comes from the infusion by the Holy Spirit of deeper faith, hope and love. And such an infusion is proportioned to one's readiness to enter into a death to the natural way of looking at oneself and the events that surround his life.

GOD AS LIGHT

This inner light makes one forget all sensible, material things. St. Symeon the New Theologian describes it as dissipating "all sufferings as so much darkness and in the repose, the light and the enjoyment of the light that suddenly makes Your Divine Spirit present to me. I recognized the tribulations as smoke . . . You are guarding me safely from wounds as You cover me with Your light."[5] This light gives strength to the contemplative to cope with all trials and tribulations that come into his life. Sufferings no longer are sufferings. One's whole value-structure becomes changed. A vision is accorded such a person of deep, interior prayer to see all things that happen as a part of God's immense love for the individual. No longer are there events or persons to be feared. Fear is to live in the darkness or absence of this glorious light that allows the individual to "know" that God is living and growing within him as he surrenders in each moment to that loving activity.

At the basis of complete abandonment in the Christian sense that is true, human creativity is the vision through faith, hope, and love of the Trinitarian Persons as loving energies shining within the contemplative and also outside within every other creature and event. This dynamic, immanent presence of the Trinity, pulsating with loving energy in all creatures, God outside of creatures and yet God inside them also, dissolves the false mask that our sinful natures place over creatures and events. We see them in God and this is the freedom of sons of God. The truth of the Word of God has truly set us free!

God is light shining within us and in all creatures. But we cannot possess Him, hold on to Him and control Him. He is "a consuming fire" (Heb 12:29). He is in process of revealing Himself. He is Yahweh who will reveal Himself in the next step, in the next event. He cannot be anticipated by man's power. He is energizing life, giving life to everything. His loving Providence extends to every little detail in the universe just as the light of the sun shines everywhere. If we do not see Him in His all-pervasive, energizing presence, it is because we are blind and are found in darkness. The light of God's loving activity is shining everywhere. We are as real and free to be ourselves as we can recognize God's loving light-presence in all things.

Thus abandonment to God's light in all events never reaches an end. For one who sees the Divine Light can never be satisfied. An inner urge burns within him to reach greater union. Thus he ardently moves forward to each event to embrace fully the presence of God as love in that moment. He looks at the same events as other people, but he sees deeper, inside, and touches the presence of God. He surrenders actively to go with that light and never step out into darkness of self-centeredness. He lives to serve God by seeking only His holy will in all things.

Even though God is the Rock, firm, stable and immovable, yet for the contemplative who abandons himself to God's loving Providence, God is always in movement. He fills all things, yet He transcends everything. He is immaterial and yet He pervades all matter. He has no mouth to speak, yet He speaks His Word within man and from inside each event. He has no hand to grasp man and guide him but man knows that God touches Him with His divine hand and raises him up in the light to gaze on His loving face. That divine hand gives an assurance, a power and a certainty that nothing can take away.

TRANSFIGURATION

Such an inner light within the contemplative showing him the loving presence of God in all events is a prelude to the full glory that awaits the Christian when he is totally transformed into Christ. This will be the face-to-face vision that will fill us with perpetual happiness that no man can ever take away. But the inner light from God even now drives out all passionate, disturbing thoughts and allows us to see God as in a mirror, in the inner self, purified from all inordinate attachments. "Blessed are the pure of heart, for they shall see God" (Mt 5:8) becomes a daily experience and the events, the adversities especially that put to death self-love, are the material that uncover the light. They become the point at which the divine light breaks as a ray of light hitting a beautifully cut diamond to scatter beauty in all directions.

This is not a naive optimism. It is rooted in the deepest faith and hope that assure the contemplative that God's process of transfiguring this material world will eventually reach a point of diaphanous presence to those who have been purified in which the whole world will be seen by the elect in the light of God's love. Abandonment is not a passive virtue of retreat but it is a call for Christians to enter into the dynamic presence of the Risen Jesus whose resurrectional presence and intercessory power are omnipotent forces within the material universe. Jesus in glory is an active leaven inserted into the mass of creation to raise the whole created world into the fullness destined for it by the Father. The whole of creation is now like a mother in agony before giving birth, groaning and laboring in pain until now (Rm 8:22).

The Christian contemplative surrenders himself freely to the Jesus "inside" of each event at each moment. He yields to His reconciling power to make all things new. He is "the First-born from the dead, the Ruler of the kings of the earth. He loves us and has washed away our sins with his blood, and made us a line of kings, priests to serve his God and Father" (Rv 1:5-6).

Such a contemplative enters into a solidarity with the Saints and angels, with the living members of the Body of Christ, the Church. He is one with the suffering world, with those who lie in darkness and have not yet seen the light. He burns actively to bring them into the light. He is humble and wants only to wash the feet of his brothers, since he has experienced his great dignity in the humility of Jesus Christ who emptied Himself, becoming obedient unto death for love of him (Ph 2:10).

To the degree that we Christians surrender ourselves freely to the leadership of Jesus Christ in each moment to allow Him to bring us, and the world through us, into a new transformation, to that degree we can say we are Christians. We will know experientially that we live in His light by the gentle love that we have toward each person that we meet at each moment. Thus we will be led from moment to moment into greater light as we see, by increased faith, hope and love, God's loving presence in all events. Complete abandonment is the Holy Spirit's gift to those who are ready to die to their false selves and begin to live in the truth of the new creatures that they are and have always been in the eyes of the Heavenly Father. Abandonment measures the reflection of Jesus Christ, the Father's Image according to whom we have all been created.

And we, with our unveiled faces reflecting like mirrors the brightness of the Lord, all grow brighter and brighter as we are turned into the image that we reflect; this is the work of the Lord who is Spirit (2 Co. 3:18).

I would like to close this book with the prayer for me and for you, the reader of these pages, that best presents what I have been trying to say in this book. These words are from the pen of J.P. De Caussade, S.J.:

O my God, when will it please you to give me the grace of remaining habitually in that union of my will with Your adorable will, in which, without our saying anything, all is said, and in which we do everything by letting You act. In this perfect union of wills we perform immense tasks because we work more in conformity with Your good pleasure; and yet we are dispensed from all toil because we place the care of everything in Your hands, and think of nothing but of reposing completely in You — a delightful state which even in the absence of all feelings of faith gives the soul an interior and altogether spiritual relish. Let me say then unceasingly through the habitual disposition of my heart, "Fiat! Yes, my God, yes, everything that You please. May Your holy desires be fulfilled in everything. I give up my own which are blind, perverse and corrupted by that miserable self-love which is the mortal enemy of Your grace and pure love, of Your glory and my own sanctification."[6]

FOOTNOTES

1. St. John of the Cross: *The Spiritual Canticle,* in: *The Collected Works of St. John of the Cross,* tr. by Kieran Kavanaugh, O.C.D. and Otilio Rodriguez, O.C.D. (Wash., D.C.: ICS Publications, Institute of Carmelite Studies, 1973) Stanza 35, p. 414.

2. Cf.: Footnote Q in the *New Jerusalem Bible* to Jn 7:38 and also what I have written in: *Bright Darkness, Jesus—The Lover of Mankind* (Denville, N.J.: Dimension Books, 1977) p. 150.

Chapter One

1. C.G. Jung: *The Archetypes and the Collective Unconscious,* Vol. 9, *Collected* Works, (Princeton: Princeton University Press, 1959-1968) p. 20.

2. T. Merton: *The Climate of Monastic Prayer,* (Spencer, Massachusetts: Cistercian Publications, 1968) p. 147.

3. T. Merton: *Conjectures of a Guilty Bystander,* (Garden City, N.Y.: Doubleday, 1965) pp. 141-42.

4. Cf.: T.M. Tomasic: "William of Saint-Thierry against Peter Abelard," in *Analecta Cisterciensia,* XXVIII, 1972, fasc. 1-2, Jan.-Dec., pp. 23-27.

Chapter Two

1. *St. Symeon the New Theologian: Hymns of Divine Love,* tr. by G.A. Maloney, S.J., (Denville, N.J.: Dimension Books, 1975) pp. 45-46.

2. Text found in Latin as quoted by T.M. Tomasic, *op. cit.,* pp. 38-39.

Chapter Four

1. St. Francis de Sales: *The Love of God*, tr. by Vincent Kerns, (Westminster, Maryland: The Newman Press, 1962) p. 416.

2. St. Augustine: De Grat, Nov. Test. seu Epist. CXL, 45.

3. St. Francis de Sales: *Spiritual Conferences*, tr. by Abbot Gasquet and Canon Mackey, O.S.B. (London: Burns & Oates Ltd., 1906) p. 282.

4. St. Augustine: *The City of God*, Bk. XVIII, ch. 13.

Chapter Five

1. St. Teresa of Avila: *Interior Castle*, tr. by E. Allison Peers, (Garden City, N.Y.: Doubleday Image Book, 1961) p. 51.

2. Francois Jamart, O.C.D.: *Complete Spiritual Doctrine of Saint Therese*, tr. by W. van de Putte, C.S.Sp., (N.Y.: St. Paul Publications, 1961) pp. 125-126.

3. St. Francis de Sales: *Treatise on the Love of God, op. cit.*, Bk. 9, ch. 9-10, pp. 385-392.

4. Dom Vital Lehodey, O.C.R.: *Holy Abandonment*, tr. by Rev. A.J. Luddy, (Dublin: M.H. Gill and Sons, Ltd., 1948) p. 8.

5. *Treatise on the Love of God*, op. cit., Bk. 8, ch. 3, p. 321.

6. J.P. De Caussade, S.J.: *Self-Abandonment to Divine Providence*, tr. by Algar Thorold, (London: Burns Oates and Washbourne Ltd., 1959) p. 5. See also Teilhard's treatment of his active and passive diminishments in his *Divine Milieu*.

7. A. Rodriguez, S.J.: *On the Practice of Christian Perfection*, tr. by J. Rickaby (Chicago, Ill.: Loyola Univ. Press, 1929) Vol. 1, pp. 523-525.

8. Bossuet: *Instruction on the States of Prayer,* cited by M. Viller in article: "Abandon," in: *Dictionnaire de Spiritualite* (Paris, G. Beauchesne, 1932) Vol. 1, col. 10.

9. St. Bernard: *In Cant. Serm.,* 83, 3.

10. St. Francis de Sales: *Treatise on the Love of God, op. cit.,* Bk. 9, ch. 5., p. 367.

11. X. De Franciosi: *L'esprit de saint Ignace* (Nancy, 1887) ch. 11, cited by M. Villers, op. cit., col. 15.

12. St. Augustine: *Sermo* 109, 13.

13. F. Jamart, *op. cit.,* p. 128.

14. J.P. De Caussade, S.J., *op. cit.,* Letter 2, pp. 110-111.

15. Dom V. Lehodey, *op. cit.,* pp. 425-460.

Chapter Six

1. Norman Pittenger: *Process Thought and Christian Faith,* (N.Y.: Macmillan, 1968) p. 13.

2. Blaise Pascal: Pensees, ed. by Brunschvieg, fragmt 172, cited by Paul Agaesse, S.J. in: "La grace du moment present," in *Christus* (Paris, 1965) Vol. 45, p. 76.

3. Teilhard de Chardin: *The Divine Milieu,* (N.Y.: Harper & Bros., Publishers, 1960) pp. 104-105.

4. R. Troisfontaine: *De L'Existence a L'Etre: La Philosophie de Gabriel Marcel,* (Namur, 1953) vol. 2, p. 48.

5. *Ibid.,* p. 201.

Chapter Seven

1. St. Basil: *The Long Rules,* in: *The Fathers of the Church Series,* I,Q.2 tr. by Sr. M. Monica Wagner, C.S.C. (Boston, Mass.: St. Paul Editions, 1950) pp. 18-25.

2. Carl Rogers: *On Becoming a Person* (Boston: Houghton-Mifflin, 1961) p. 90.

3. Martin Buber: *I and Thou* (N.Y.: Charles Scribner's Sons, 1958) p. 248.

Chapter Eight

1. J.P. De Caussade, S.J., *op. cit.*, letter 1, pp. 298-99.

2. Adrian Van Kaam: *Religion and Personality,* (Englewood Cliffs, N.J.: Prentice Hall, Inc., 1964) pp. 92-101.

3. Thomas a Kempis: *The Imitation of Christ,* Bk. 1; ch. 12.

4. St. Basil: *In Julittam,* 4; *PG* 32; 245A.

Chapter Nine

1. Karl Rahner: *Theological Investigations,* tr. by David Bourke, Vol. VII, (N.Y.: Herder & Herder, 1971) p. 15.

2. St. John of the Cross: *The Ascent of Mount Carmel,* Bk. 2, ch. 13, in: *The Collected Works of St. John of the Cross,* tr. by Kieran Kavanaugh, O.C.D. and Otilio Rodriguez, O.C.D. (Wash. D.C.: ICS Publications, Institute of Carmelite Studies, 1973) pp. 140-141.

3. St. John of the Cross: *The Dark Night, op. cit.,* p. 313.

4. Pseudo-Dionysius: *Mystical Theology,* cited in: *The Soul Afire,* ed. by H.A. Reinhold (Garden City, N.Y.: Doubleday, Image Books, 1973) p. 49.

5. Leonard Boase, S.J.: *The Prayer of Faith*, (St. Louis: B. Herder Book Co., 1962) p. 93.

6. Hugh of St. Victor, cited in: *The Soul Afire*, *op. cit.*, p. 290.

7. St. John of the Cross: *The Dark Night*, Bk. 2, ch. 3, *op. cit.*, p. 333.

8. George A. Maloney, S.J.: *The Breath of the Mystic*, (Denville, N.J.: Dimensions Books, 1974) p. 54.

9. St. John of the Cross: *The Living Flame of Love*, Stanza 3, 39, *op. cit.*, p. 625.

10. V. Lehodey, *op. cit.*, pp. 361-362.

11. See: G.A. Maloney, S.J.: *Man, the Divine Icon*, (Pecos, N.M.: Dove Publications, 1973), especially Chapter 8 on St. Gregory Nyssa, pp. 133-160.

12. St. Gregory of Nyssa: *Homilia in Canticum* XV, *PG* 44, 1085 B-C.

13. St. John of the Cross: *The Living Flame of Love*, *op. cit.*, pp. 578-579.

14. St. Gregory of Nyssa: *De Beatitudine*, Or. VII, *PG* 44, 1280 B-C.

EPILOGUE: FOOTNOTES

1. *Fifty Spiritual Homilies of St. Macarius the Egyptian*, tr. and ed. by D. Mason, S.J., (N.Y.: Macmillan Co., 1921) Homily 15, pp. 22, 43.

2. Julian Green: *Journal*, T. 1-7, (Paris: Plon, 1928-1958) p. 439.

3. St. John of the Cross: *The Spiritual Canticle,* Stanza 11, *op. cit.,* p. 411.

4. Macarius of Egypt: *Fifty Spiritual Homilies, op. cit.,* Homily 50, 2.

5. Cited in: G.A. Maloney, S.J.: *The Mystic of Fire and Light, St. Symeon the New Theologian,* (Denville, N.J.: Dimension Books, 1975) p. 95.

6. J.P. De Caussade, *op. cit.,* p. 449.